MW01707160

The ACT Black Book

Score-Raising Strategies for the ACT

2009 – 2010 Edition

By: Nicholas A. LaMantia

SuperiorTestPrep.com **ACTBlackBook.com**

Hello, and welcome to The ACT Black Book. You are clearly interested in improving your ACT score, and this book will help maximize your results. I have developed the strategies in this book while working as a tutor for a small, private company near Chicago. The company has to keep waiting lists due to the stories of our students' successes; not bad considering we do not advertise and charge a premium price of $100 per hour.

During my time as a private tutor, I have reviewed many ACT preparation books. I have found these books only marginally helpful at best. In fact, some give blatantly bad advice. Good tutors know the tips that really make a difference in your ACT score, but these tips have not yet been collected anywhere. So, I put all my proven tricks and strategies into the next 85 pages. There is no need to settle for an ineffective book or to pay hundreds of dollars for tutoring; by using my tips, working hard, and developing a strategy, you will perform to the best of your ability on test day. A little bit of work now will go a long way towards getting the college acceptances and scholarships you deserve.

Table of Contents

Introduction and FAQ

The ACT Test has worried students for 50 years now. One test with so much on the line can be quite nerve-wracking, right? Well you can worry about it a little - that's only healthy - but there is no need to freak out. First of all, your high school grades and classes will be the most important part of your college applications, so keep working in the classroom. Secondly, the ACT can be taken as many times as you wish, and at the current rate of $32 per test (the optional Writing Test adds $15 more), it is not all that expensive to give it another go. Finally, through practice and good advice, anyone can earn a solid score on the ACT. Relax and do your best.

Some common questions students have:

What will I be tested on? How long does the testing take?

The ACT is a multiple choice test with four separate sections called "subtests". The four subtests are labeled English, Math, Reading, and Science. Each subtest has a time limit of between 35 and 60 minutes. Overall you will be taking about three hours of tests, but the whole process takes about four hours including breaks and the reading of directions. You may also take the optional Writing Test, which is a 30 minute test given about 15 minutes after the four subtests are completed.

When is the test offered and how do I sign up?

ACT offers one "national test day" each February, April, June, September, October, and December. Additionally, some states organize a statewide test day for high school juniors to take the ACT during school hours. The statewide tests are usually administered in March or April.

The sign up deadline for a national test day is roughly a month before the day of the exam. See *ACTstudent.org* for exact schedules. You can register late (up to about two or three weeks before test time), but you will be required to pay an extra fee. Registration for the statewide test day is generally handled by the student's high school.

What is the story with the optional Writing Test? Should I take it?

The optional Writing Test gives you 30 minutes to compose a written response to a question or "prompt" chosen by ACT. You will not know the prompt until you begin the test, but the subject of the prompt always relates to high school life. More detailed information on the format of the Writing Test can be found on page 73 of this book.

You probably should take the optional Writing Test. It is being recommended or required by more and more colleges each year. You can check on *ACTstudent.org/writing* or on official college websites to find a specific university's policy for the Writing Test. Even if your college does not require the test, it still shows good initiative to take it. Plus, by using my tips you should have no problem getting a decent score, even if writing is not your strongest subject.

What is the scoring scale for the ACT? What is a good score?

The four subtests of the ACT are each graded on a 1 – 36 scale, with 36 being the best possible score. You also receive a composite score, which averages the scores of your four subtests into one overall score on a 1 – 36 scale. The national average for the composite score is roughly a 21. Pages 73 and 74 include scoring details for the Writing Test.

Although this may sound cheesy, a "good score" is the score you receive when you perform to the best of your own abilities. If you got a 28, but you did not prepare for the test and stayed out late the night before taking it, you really did not get a good score. With a little hard work you could have scored in the 30s and put yourself in line for scholarship money. If you got a 19, and you worked hard to prepare for the test, then you did get a good score. Maybe you improved from a 16 and now can attend a four year university instead of the local community college.

How are the individual subtests graded?

You receive a score based solely on the number of questions you get correct. No extra penalty is assessed for incorrect answers. The exact grading scale changes from test to test because every test is graded on a curve. For example, on an easier test you may get 45 questions correct on the Math section and receive a 24. On a harder test, 45 questions correct might be scored as a 27. Your score depends on how you performed in comparison to the other students throughout the country who took the test that day.

How is my composite (overall) score determined?

Your composite score is determined by averaging the scores you receive on each of the four subtests (English, Math, Reading, and Science). The Writing score and the Writing / English score do not affect your composite score at all. These scores are presented in addition to the composite if you choose to take the Writing Test.

The test was harder / easier than the practice exam. What gives?

Every test is different. Sometimes the Reading section is a breeze, and sometimes it is full of complicated language. Sometimes you don't see any advanced trigonometry on the

Math section; sometimes you see three questions on it. It's the luck of the draw. Just remember, it's all graded on a curve, so harder tests mean easier grading standards.

I heard it's easier to get a high score on the September / April / June / etc. test. Is that true?

Some students do slightly better on June's version, but it really does not make much of a difference. June stands out a little because many students who are happy with their composite scores of 25 or 29 or 33 are done taking the ACT by June. This leaves out some of the students who would stretch the curve. However, do not count on a big jump just because it's June! It only makes a slight difference.

How many times should I take the test?

Take the test two to four times. Nearly 60% percent of students see a rise in their score from their first to second test. And if your score stays the same or drops, no big deal, <u>you only report your best score to colleges anyway</u>. If you are happy with your score after your second try, that's good enough. If you think you can do better or are shooting for a scholarship or reach school, try it a third or fourth time. Taking it five or more times is fine, but you will probably not make any significant gains by then.

Can I get my answer / question sheet back?

For certain national test days, you can pay $17 for a "Test Information Release (TIR)". The TIR includes a copy of the questions, your answers, and the correct answers. Lately this service has only been offered for the December, April, and June tests. Check *ACTstudent.org/scores/release* for specific details. <u>If you think you may take the ACT again at some point, order the TIR. It is very helpful to review your test, go over questions you missed, and determine the areas in which you need more practice.</u> Your TIR can be ordered through *ACTstudent.org* during registration or up to three months after the test day.

How many correct answers do I need for a certain score?

Again, it depends on the curve. Generally, for every one or two questions you miss on a section you lose a point. Here are a few figures from the official scoring for a recent ACT Test to give you an idea:

English – 75 questions total
70 correct = 31 ; 65 correct = 27 ; 55 correct = 23 ; 45 correct = 19 ; 35 correct = 15

Math – 60 questions total
55 correct = 33 ; 50 correct = 29 ; 40 correct = 24 ; 30 correct = 19 ; 20 correct = 16

Reading – 40 questions total
35 correct = 31 ; 30 correct = 26 ; 25 correct = 21 ; 20 correct = 18 ; 15 correct = 15

Science – 40 questions total
35 correct = 32 ; 30 correct = 27 ; 25 correct = 23 ; 20 correct = 20 ; 15 correct = 18

The Math on this particular ACT was a bit more difficult than usual, so the curve is fairly generous. The other subtest curves are around their respective averages. Exact numbers will fluctuate from test to test.

I took the test already, but now I want to go up two points in my composite score. What do I need to do?

You will need to get about 9 – 18 more questions correct throughout the entire test. Remember that your composite score is an average of your four scores on the subtests. If you work hard to bring your Math score up four points, but all your other tests stay the same, your composite score only rises one point. Be well-rounded and work on every section, whether it is a strength or a weakness. The goal is simply to get more questions correct!

How do I send scores to colleges? Can I select which scores I report from different test days?

First of all, you cannot send certain sections from certain days. You have to send the entire ACT score report for a given day. With that said, if in October you got a 17 overall and in April you got a 21, you do not need to tell the college your October score. Send only the April report. You can send the official reports to colleges through the ACT website. You can also arrange to have reports automatically sent to colleges when you register for the test. However, with this option you will not be able to see your score before the college does, so I do not recommend it.

Note: If you have other questions regarding the basics of the ACT, log on to www.ACTstudent.org/FAQ. It contains a comprehensive FAQ about registering for the test, score reporting, special accommodations, and more.

How to Use your ACT Black Book – Preparing for the ACT Test

First of all, I recommend that you supplement this book with two to four practice tests. This book has many practice questions, but it is more of a strategy guide. **It is extremely helpful to sit down and take complete practice tests.** Practice test books are inexpensive online or at book stores, and they often are available for free at your school or local library. I strongly recommend practice tests from ACT, Inc (the creators of the ACT Test), which are most readily found in the "*Real ACT*" series of books. ***ACTstudent.org/sampletest* contains one free practice test from ACT, Inc that can get you started.** After studying your ACT Black Book and completing a few practice tests, you will be completely prepared for the ACT.

The key to getting the most from your ACT study time (or any study time) is a concept I call "Active Preparation". Active Preparation does not mean you must spend months studying for the ACT. Actually, roughly 15 – 35 hours of total preparation time should be adequate. Active Preparation simply means that your brain is constantly working during your study time; it is making connections and intently trying to learn new concepts. Active Preparation is scientifically proven to be more effective than simply trying to memorize. Results come quickly with an "active" approach.

So how does The ACT Black Book fit into Active Preparation? The ACT Black Book is short, but loaded with strategies. When I tutor students, I go over the strategies in this book many times. Consequently, this book is not designed to be read once and put away. Read through it slowly and highlight passages you find especially helpful. Write down notes (each chapter ends with two blank pages for notes) and always be thinking of ways you can apply the tricks and tips to test questions. As you correct practice tests, keep this book open and find connections between the practice questions and the tips from this book. Finally, review this book and any notes you have as your test date approaches.

When reviewing practice tests, the concept of Active Preparation also comes into play. "Actively" correct practice problems and previous ACT Tests you have taken. Don't just mark something wrong and move on! Study the correct answer and try to understand why you got the question wrong. Learn from your mistakes so you do not make them again on the next test. Analyzing a practice test you took is a much better way to spend a couple hours than just mindlessly moving on to another test. The goal is to learn something!

Note: You do not have to take an entire practice test in one sitting – this would take three hours. Taking one section at a time is perfectly fine.

General ACT Tips – A few pointers to use throughout the test

- Don't leave anything blank! There is no extra penalty for wrong answers.

- **Don't spend too much time on any one question. Every question, hard or easy, is worth the same amount of points.** If you are struggling with a question, circle it and come back at the end if you have time. You don't want to miss the last five questions because you wasted time on one really tough one.

- When working on a question, cross out answers that you are sure are incorrect. It always helps to narrow things down to clear your thinking and improve your chances when making a guess.

- Guessing on the last few questions is preferable to speeding through the last five minutes trying to finish every question. I see a lot of students start rushing on the last ten questions, and end up getting them all wrong. It would be better to do six of these at a good pace, and then just guess on the last four.

- Use my tips, but also use your brain. Not every question will fit squarely into one of my tips and tricks. You have been going to school and taking tests for many years; use that knowledge as well!

- Be prepared. This doesn't mean you need to study for months or spend hundreds of dollars on tutoring. But knowing the test format and having a strategy going into the test will improve your score considerably.

- Be in peak condition on test day. A colleague of mine used to say, "In five years you will not remember what you did on Friday night before the ACT, but you will remember your ACT score." Stay in and get a good night's rest before test day. Eat a solid breakfast of protein-rich foods (sugary foods can make you crash midway through the test). Have pencils and calculators ready to go. Being prepared calms your nerves and gives you confidence. You can go out and celebrate after the test!

- Stay calm and cool. Panicking because of pressure or lack of time will not help anything. Remember, you can always retake the test if things go wrong.

Chapter 1 – English

English is the easiest section to improve upon. Spend some time working on it. If you have never taken an ACT English Test, try at least two passages from a practice test before getting into the "The Basic Tips" section on page 11. The free test given at *ACTstudent.org/sampletest* will work fine.

Format and Basic Strategy

The English section focuses on grammar, sentence structure, and general organization. The section contains five short passages, each with 15 questions interspersed throughout the text. The format for most questions is that ACT underlines part of a passage and then expects you to correct any errors made. Here's a quick example just to illustrate the question format:

Jim went to Puerto <u>Rico, for the first time, in</u> 1935.

A. No Change
B. Rico, for the first time in
C. Rico for the first time in
D. Rico for the first time, in

"No Change" means that you are choosing to leave the text as it is. The correct answer is C.

Some questions give some further directions instead of just having you edit the underlined text. I refer to these as "worded questions" because they actually ask a question in words. For example, a worded question may look like this:

Which statement would fit best given the information from the preceding sentence?

A. Jim likes to travel.
B. Jim has never been out of Canada.
C. Jim has lived in Puerto Rico his whole life.
D. Jim was born in 1775.

The correct answer is A.

Overall, you are given 45 minutes to complete 75 questions. This gives you 36 seconds per question. It does not sound like a lot, but English questions generally don't take long to complete. Chances are you will have more time than you think. Practice and find a comfortable pace for yourself.

The Basic Tips

1. *Read Everything*

Unless you have problems finishing the English section in the allotted time, it is best to read the entire passage as you go along. It is tempting to skip sentences that do not have questions in them, but you will do better overall if you read them anyway. Reading everything enables you to understand the passage better, which is helpful on many questions.

2. *Go with the Simplest Answer*

If the simplest answer fits in the sentence, go with it. The ACT constantly asks questions that test your ability to keep text brief and to the point. For students who are in the 16 – 20 range in English, this tip alone can bring a score to the low 20s. For those strong in English, just keep this tip in mind; it is extremely useful. Here are a few common examples of this tip:

We sat on the plane, eager to start our long flight <u>north, a lengthy journey.</u>

A. No Change
B. north, a long tour.
C. north, many miles away.
D. north.

The correct answer is D. They already mentioned that it is a long flight. We don't need to say that it is lengthy or far away again. **Never add extra words unless they present genuinely new and important information.** If you are unsure about an answer, opt to keep the text brief and simple. About 85% of the time ACT wants you to remove words, not add them.

(From a passage about Albert Einstein's life) Einstein became interested in physics at an early <u>age, as did noted physicist Enrico Fermi.</u> Einstein began reading scientific texts when he was only ten.

A. No Change
B. age.
C. age, though his brother preferred the arts.
D. age, but we don't know the exact year.

The correct answer is B. The other information is not relevant to the main focus of the passage, so there is no need to include it. Again, we want to keep the text brief and the sentence structure simple.

> Wild animals can be dangerous to anyone, even trained handlers, that is why learning to spot tracks is essential to hikers.
>
> A. No Change
> B. handlers and
> C. handlers, who say
> D. handlers. That is why

The correct answer is D. This example uses the *Go with the Simplest Answer* tip in a slightly different way than just eliminating extra text. The simplest method to connect thoughts is by adding a period and forming two sentences. If you can separate the original sentence into two simple sentences that make sense, it will always be correct.

3. *Don't be Afraid to Choose "No Change" or "Delete the underlined portion"*

It is a common mistake that students are less likely to choose "No Change" or "Delete the underlined portion" than any other answer choice. Don't think this way! "No Change" is just as good an answer as any other, as is "Delete the underlined portion." In fact, if "Delete" (sometimes "Omit" is used instead) is an answer choice, see if that choice works first. It is often the correct answer.

4. *Read the Whole Sentence when Answering the Question*

Another common mistake that students make is that they only read up to the underlined portion of the sentence, and then try to answer the question. Sometimes an answer seems correct at this point, but becomes wrong when the rest of the sentence is taken into account. **Read the whole sentence before choosing an answer.** In fact, if you are unsure of the answer, **try inserting each choice into the sentence and reading the resulting sentence from start to finish.** Pay attention to this tip as you try the following examples.

There are the senior citizens who are reliving the music of their generation, to the teenagers who have just discovered the style, the Uptown Jazz Festival sells thousands of tickets each year.

A. No Change
B. From
C. One can see
D. Delete the underlined portion

The correct answer is B. It is easy to make a mistake on this type of question if you don't read all the way to the period before choosing an answer.

The design worked out well as he created his first guitar – and his young life's dream – he knew his grandpa was looking on.

A. No Change
B. well, as
C. well. As
D. well,

The correct answer is C. I modeled this example after a question that 70% of my students got wrong on their first try. Only by reading all the way through to the period can you understand why separating it into two sentences is correct. Remember, separating it into two simple sentences is always preferable to using commas (at least in the eyes of the ACT graders).

5. *Don't Get Carried Away with the Commas*

Students tend to put in too many commas. If you are unsure, chances are no comma should be used. This tip is especially helpful to those who score under a 23 in English.

Jenny was smart but inattentive. She occasionally made thoughtless mistakes.

A. No Change
B. smart, but inattentive.
C. smart.
D. smart, but, inattentive.

The correct answer is A. There is no pause in this sentence, so no comma is needed. The technical reason is because "inattentive" is not an independent clause, but I prefer to think of it using the next tip (#6).

Note: If you are really good with grammatical rules, these rules certainly can be used to solve English questions. However, if you are not a wiz with grammatical rules, I would avoid concentrating on them; there are many exceptions that can get you into trouble.

Note 2: The above question is an example where the shortest, simplest option (C) <u>is not</u> the correct answer. Why? The word "inattentive" presents new information that is needed to understand the passage, so it cannot be deleted.

6. *Pretend You are Saying the Sentence to a Friend*

When you are unsure about using a comma, **say the sentence out loud like you are talking to a friend**. If you pause in a spot, chances are that is the place for a comma. If you do not pause, no comma is used. You will be surprised how well this works. Of course, you will have to pretend to say the sentence aloud during quiet test time.

This tip works best with comma questions, but it can also be used on just about any other question. In fact, I have known a few successful students who took this approach to answering nearly every single question on the English Test. As you attempt to solve the following question, pretend you are saying each answer choice out loud to a friend during a casual conversation.

> Adams always thought her best success was raising her son James, <u>who was a Yale graduate and who also was good at athletics.</u>
>
> A. No change
> B. a sporty Yale man.
> C. who was a Yale graduate and an accomplished athlete.
> D. who was a man who excelled in athletics and also managed to graduate from Yale University.

The correct answer is C. Choices A, B, and D would make this sentence sound somewhat awkward if you were to say it during a casual conversation. Choice C refrains from using extra words and unclear language. It sounds like the way you would say the sentence when talking to a friend.

7. *Answer Only the Question They Ask*

This tip applies only to "worded questions" (see page 10 for a definition). You generally see about ten to fifteen of these questions per test, and they probably are the most common type of English question that students answer incorrectly. **The trick to these**

questions is to answer ONLY what they ask. Don't even worry about which answer seems to fit the passage best. This is best illustrated through the following examples.

> The climate of California's coastline varies from the mild north to the hot southern tip of the state. <u>The northwest contains more forests and wooded areas than the south.</u>
>
> Given that all the choices are true, which sentence provides the most specific support for the preceding sentence?
>
> A. No Change
> B. Summer highs in Los Angeles (Southern CA) reach around 85° F, while San Francisco (Northern CA) only hits roughly 70° F.
> C. The Southern coast is a great place for surfing and water sports.
> D. My favorite city in California is San Diego.

The correct answer is B. This sentence may not sound the best at first, but remember, we are answering ONLY what the question asks. ACT wants specific support for the preceding sentence, which focuses on climate differences within California. Answer B gives specific information which directly supports the preceding sentence.

Note: You can take this approach to solve any "worded question," especially ones that say "given that all the choices are true" in them. Just remember your job is to answer ONLY what the question asks. These questions are <u>not</u> designed to test grammar or to have you determine which sentence sounds best in the passage.

I will give one more example of this type of question as a lead-in to Tip 8:

… He is married to Midge, a homemaker, and they have three children: the mischievous Burt, the smart Lena, and the lovable baby Margaret. Together they make up a classic television family.

The family lives in the town of Sprungfeld. Hilarious personalities such as Matt, the unlucky bartender, and Kricky, the cynical entertainer, provide some of the funniest moments…

Given that all the choices are true, which sentence most effectively leads from the subject of the preceding paragraph to the subject of this one?

A. No Change
B. Many characters are featured in the show.
C. The family interacts with a large cast of entertaining characters.
D. The show has continued for many years due to its outstanding writing.

The correct answer is C. C is the only choice that mentions the family (subject of the last paragraph) and supporting characters (subject of this paragraph). That is exactly what the question asks for, and thus C is the correct choice. This example also connects to my next tip…

8. *Don't Answer Questions Until You Have All the Information*

When in doubt read more; you will only get a better understanding of the question. For example, **if a question asks about the next paragraph, don't answer the question until you have read that paragraph or at least skimmed through to find the answer.** Some students circle these questions then return to them after reading the needed information.

Furthermore, at the end of each passage ACT usually asks a general question about the passage as a whole. Don't be afraid to go back and review what you've read. Sometimes just looking back at the title of the passage can give you valuable information for the end-of-passage questions.

Some Common Question Types

1. *Order Questions*

The ACT often contains questions asking if the order of sentences or paragraphs should be changed to improve the passage. These questions always have some distinct clue to the correct answer. Often it is as easy as a progression of time (for example, the character ages, years pass, etc.); sometimes you have to look further. Take a little extra time on "Order Questions" and look for a clear reason for the sequence of sentences or paragraphs.

2. *Possessive Questions*

Many students struggle with these questions. All "Possessive Questions" will ask you to pick from " 's "   " s' " and " s ". I'll explain a technique to solve them through two short examples.

My <u>neighbor's house</u> is decorated for Christmas.

A. No Change
B. neighbors' house
C. neighbors house
D. neighbors' houses

The correct answer is A. To solve Possessive Questions, take the second word ("house"), and say "Whose house is it?" If the word before ("neighbor") answers that question, you know an apostrophe will be needed. Now you need to determine where to put the apostrophe. The next question to ask is "How many neighbors are we talking about?" Here we are talking about one, so you use "neighbor's". If the sentence read "My neighbors' houses are decorated for Christmas." we would be talking about more than one neighbor, so you would use the s'.

A slightly trickier example...

The Western College Football Conference has 11 teams. Each <u>teams' mascot</u> is different.

A. No Change
B. team's mascot
C. teams mascot
D. teams mascot,

The correct answer is B. Whose mascot is it? The team's; so you need an apostrophe. How many teams are we talking about? One; so you use "team's".... But wait we just said there are 11 teams, right? Well, that's true, but it says "each team" in the sentence, so we really are only talking about one team here. Watch out for this kind of tricky wording!

3. *Which One is NOT Acceptable Questions*

Generally there are two to four questions per test that ask, "Which of the following alternatives to the underlined portion would NOT be acceptable?" Sometimes the wording or format is changed slightly, but these questions all share one trait: one answer choice is blatantly not acceptable. This choice will always have a serious error in grammar or syntax (choice of words). So don't choose an answer because it sounds kind of weird. Choose the answer that, for example, creates a fragmented sentence that is not grammatically correct (remember we are choosing what is NOT acceptable). Spend a little extra time on these questions and try to find the answer that clearly is not acceptable. I'll give an example.

Jim sold his insurance business to Jane Smith in <u>2004, after concluding</u> that he preferred the life of a musician.

Which of the following alternatives to the underlined portion would NOT be acceptable?

A. 2004 after his conclusion
B. 2004 upon concluding
C. 2004. He had concluded
D. 2004. Concluding

The correct answer is D. "Concluding that he preferred the life of a musician." is not a complete sentence. Although they don't all sound perfect, the other choices all form complete thoughts. D is the only choice that is unacceptable.

4. *Consistency of Person or Tense Questions*

These questions are common on the ACT. They are not the most difficult type, but recognizing them will prevent you from making mistakes. Check out the examples.

Karl Benz soon invented the gas-powered automobile, an open air two-seater with .75 horsepower. About ten years after inventing autos, Karl <u>has started</u> to make a living selling them to consumers.

A. No Change
B. would have started
C. had started
D. have started

The correct answer is C. We are in the past tense here, which we can see from the previous sentence and the subject of the essay. When you see questions like this, remember the tip **when in doubt read more**. Look to the previous sentence, the next sentence, and to the subject of the essay to find clues about which tense to use. These questions can be relatively easy if you approach them correctly.

> Stanley found the movie-making business to be his true passion. Set designs and optical illusions were its specialty.

A. No Change
B. his
C. their
D. Delete the underlined portion

The correct answer is B. You need to use clues from the last sentence to make sure you choose the correct pronoun. These examples may seem easy to you, but the goal is to learn to recognize these questions. They are harder to notice when you are in the midst of a test.

5. *Transition Word Questions*

By transition words I mean words like "however," "on the other hand," "therefore," etc. that usually come at the beginning of a sentence. This is another situation where you must read the previous sentence to determine which word makes sense – you have to find the purpose for the transition word.

Often times these questions will give you the option to delete the transition word(s) altogether. "Delete" is very commonly the correct choice. Don't leave the transition word in the text unless it is absolutely necessary to the paragraph making sense. I'll give two short examples.

> My first trip to Rome included visits to the Coliseum, Pantheon, and other ancient structures. Consequently, I was amazed by the complex beauty of these giant buildings.

A. No Change
B. However,
C. Therefore,
D. Delete the underlined portion

The correct answer is D. Try reading the sentences after deleting the underlined portion; notice how everything still makes perfect sense. There is no need for a transition word to clarify the meaning of the sentences.

> Bill Walton announces several professional basketball games each week. Therefore, he had a problem with stuttering as a child.
>
> A. No Change
> B. However,
> C. In addition,
> D. Delete the underlined portion

The correct answer is B. Here we need "however" because we have two contrasting sentences. Without a transition word the reader may get confused. But remember, unless there is a clear need for a transition, as in this example, you should choose to delete the transition word(s).

6. *"Setting Off" with Commas Questions*

I mentioned that generally there are too many commas. However, sometimes you will have to add one to the text. One common place is in a sentence that looks like the following example.

> We saw Jim Henderson the local blacksmith, run to put out the fire.
>
> A. No Change
> B. Henderson the local blacksmith
> C. Henderson, the local blacksmith
> D. Henderson, the local blacksmith,

The correct answer is D. In this example we could pull out the words "the local blacksmith" and this would still be a grammatically correct sentence. When this is the case, you "set that phrase off" by commas (put one on either side). Alternatively, sometimes the ACT uses dashes to "set off" phrases. Dashes function the exact same way as commas. Just make sure you either have two dashes or two commas setting the phrase off, not one of each.

A Few Grammatical Rules to Know

- *Its, its', it's and who's, whose*

  " Its' " is not a real word. " It's " means "it is," and I have yet to see ACT use a contraction as a correct answer. These choices will always be wrong. When asked to choose between these three options, t**he answer is always " its ".**

  "Whose" is the possessive form of "who". "Who's" means "who is," and contractions are not used as correct answers.

- *Semicolons*

  Just think of a semicolon as a period. It functions the exact same way.

- *Colons*

  On the ACT, colons are usually only used to start a list. Notice how the following example would not sound correct if you removed the colon.

  > I ate the following foods for lunch: an apple, a cheeseburger and potato chips.

  But if the phrase works as a sentence without the colon, you don't need to add one. Notice how the following example sounds perfectly fine without a colon. There is no need for one here.

  > For lunch I ate an apple, a cheeseburger and potato chips.

- *Who vs. Whom*

  I have never seen "whom" be the correct answer on any ACT Test. Technically "whom" is used only when it is the object of a sentence, as in "You went to the dance with whom?" Stick with "who" unless you are completely sure "whom" is correct.

- *Then vs. Than*

  "Than" is used in comparisons, as in "Nick is faster than Jack. "Then" has a few meanings that usually have to do with the passing of time. Just remember, if it's a comparison use "than".

- *Began vs. Begun, Sang vs. Sung, Rang vs. Rung, etc.*

  You only use begun, sung, or rung when a form of the word "have" or "was" is in front of it. Otherwise you use began, sang, or rang. Here are a few sentences illustrating the difference:

  > Jim had sung his whole life. On that dreary day he sang better than he ever had before.

  > We began the test at three o'clock. The bell was rung a few hours later.

End of Section Note: The strategies presented in this section are designed to supplement the knowledge you already have. If you're taking the ACT, you have some smarts. Use them! These tips will apply to most questions in one way or another, but don't try to find a trick for every single question. Think each question through and do your best. Finally, the more you practice, the better you will do. I recommend trying at least two sample English Tests before you sit for the real thing.

Notes - English

Notes - English

Chapter 2 – Math

Try a practice test after reading this chapter. You can reference the formulas on pages 27 – 31 while taking practice tests; just make sure you memorize them before you take the real thing.

Format and Basic Strategy

The Math section tests a wide range of algebra concepts, some geometry, and a small amount of trigonometry. You get 60 minutes to complete 60 questions. **Math questions start easy and get harder as the test goes on.** For example, #20 is harder than #1, #30 is harder than #20, and so on. Use your time wisely; if you find #40 – #60 to be extremely difficult, spend extra time on the earlier questions and make sure you get those correct. If you believe you can solve the harder questions, save time for them by getting through the easier questions quickly. Just watch out for "stupid mistakes"! **Practice and have a strategy going into the test.**

This section contains more formulas and academic information than the others. The Fact is, you need to know certain formulas and mathematical concepts to excel in this section. Formulas are found on pages 27 to 31. I strongly recommend memorizing them prior to test time. Pages 32 to 36 focus on tips and tricks. Finally, pages 37 to 44 contain practice problems that reinforce some concepts. Pages 45 and 46 are left blank for your notes on this section.

Because students have wide ranges of mathematical ability, I rank each practice question on a scale of 1 (easiest) to 6 (most difficult). If math is not a strength for you, don't worry if the higher difficulty questions are puzzling. The 5 and 6 difficulty questions are designed for students shooting to score in the high 20s or 30s. Give every question an honest try, though. You may learn something that helps you on test day.

Lastly, most calculators are allowed on the Math section. I recommend using a TI-83 Plus or TI-84 Plus calculator because they are user friendly, have a large display, and are capable of performing all the necessary mathematical functions. Most of the older TI models also work fine.

No rules prohibit programming formulas into your calculator. At my website *www.ACTCalculatorFormulas.com* I offer a service in which you send me your TI-83 Plus or TI-84 Plus calculator and I program roughly 30 different formulas and automatic solvers into it. I also sell brand new calculators that come preloaded with the programs. The programs walk you through certain calculations that are common on the ACT. It is best to memorize the formulas, but if you think you may forget a few, my programs can be quite helpful.

See *ACTstudent.org* for full calculator rules.

The Math formulas you will use on nearly every test:

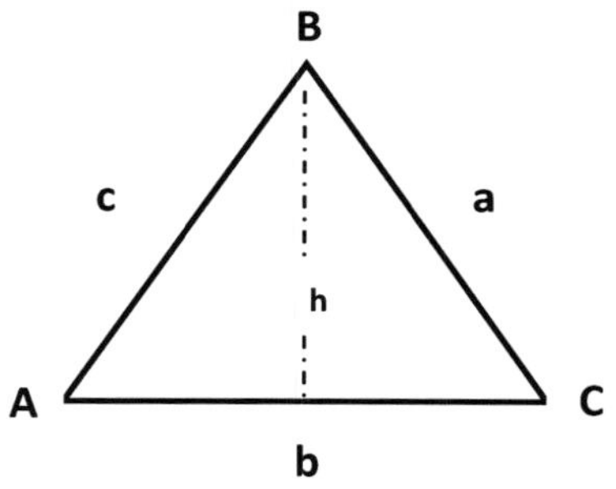

<u>Triangles</u>

Area $=$ ½(base x height)

The 3 angles add to 180^0

$\text{Sin}\frac{\angle A}{a} = \text{Sin}\frac{\angle B}{b} = \text{Sin}\frac{\angle C}{c}$

Note: This formula will be given to you on the test if it is needed, but it helps to be familiar with it anyway.

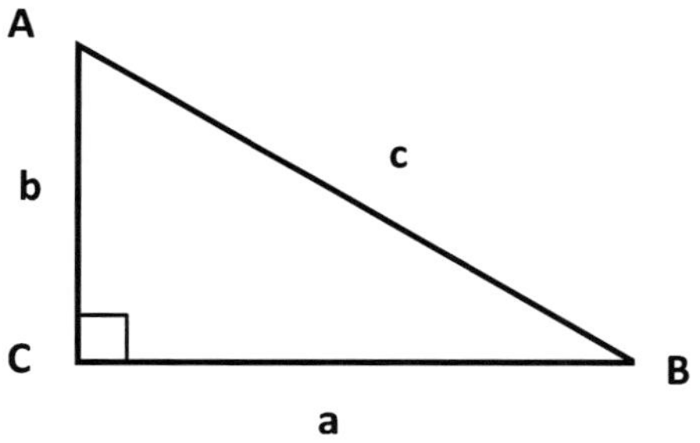

<u>Right Triangles:</u> (contain a 90^0 angle)

All formulas above apply here as well

Pythagorean Theorem: $a^2 + b^2 = c^2$

<u>Special Triangles:</u>

45 – 45 – 90

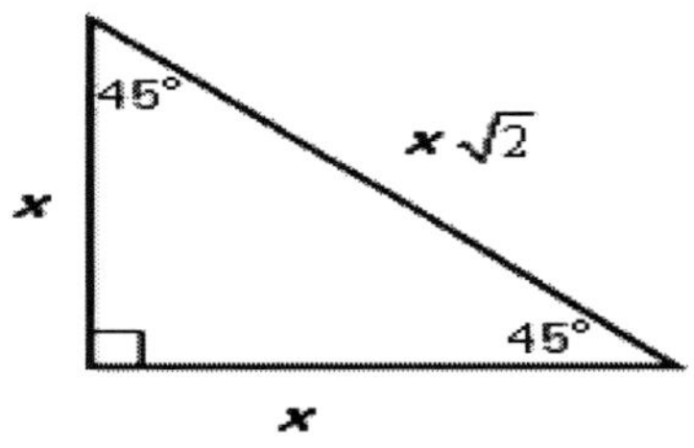

So if one leg = 3, the other leg = 3, and the hypotenuse = $3\sqrt{2}$

30 – 60 – 90

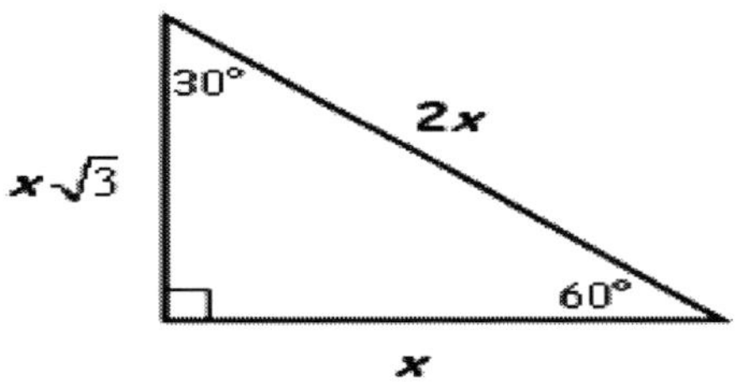

So if the smaller leg = 2, the other leg = $2\sqrt{3}$, and the hypotenuse = 4

<u>Equilateral Triangle</u> – All sides are the same length, all angles are 60^0

<u>Isosceles Triangle</u> – Two sides are the same length; the angles opposite these two sides are the same; The 45 – 45 – 90 triangle is an example of an isosceles triangle

Similar Triangles – Two different triangles with the same angle measures; their side lengths will be proportional

Example: All sides on the second triangle are ½ the length of the sides on the first triangle

Notice how all angle measures are identical

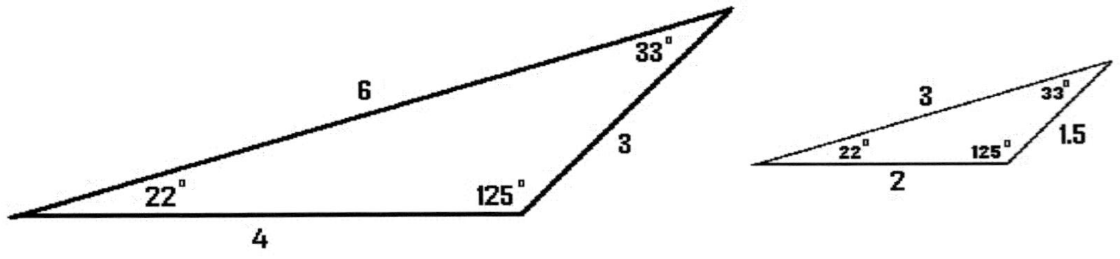

SOH CAH TOA – a law of any right triangle

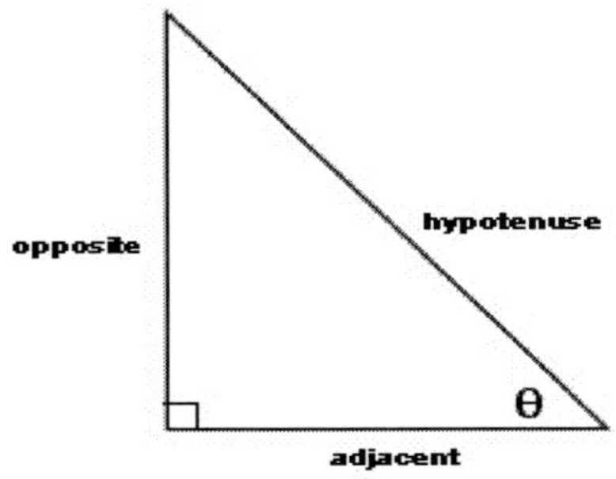

SOH $\sin\theta = \text{Opposite} \div \text{Hypotenuse}$

CAH $\cos\theta = \text{Adjacent} \div \text{Hypotenuse}$

TOA $\tan\theta = \text{Opposite} \div \text{Adjacent}$

"Opposite" refers to the length of the side across from the angle in question

"Adjacent" refers to the length of the side next to the angle in question

"Hypotenuse" refers to the length of the side across from the 90° angle

Circles

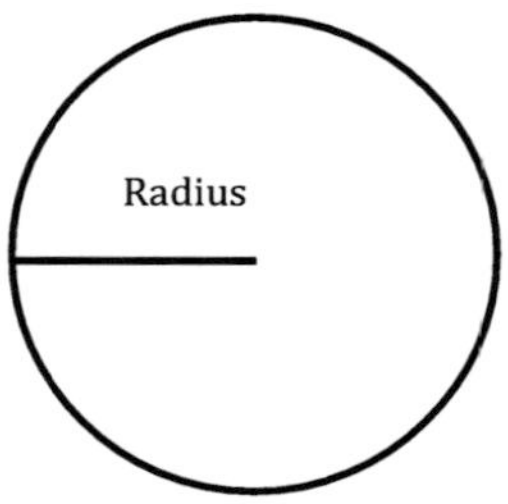

Equation of a circle = $(x-h)^2 + (y-k)^2 = r^2$

r is the radius, h and k are the x and y points of the center respectively

Example: $(x-4)^2 + (y+3)^2 = 100$

This would be a circle centered at (4,-3) with a radius of 10

Area of a circle = πr^2 Circumference of a circle = $2\pi r$

A full circle = 360^0 or 2π radians

Other Geometric Shapes

Squares

Area = S x S

Perimeter = 4S

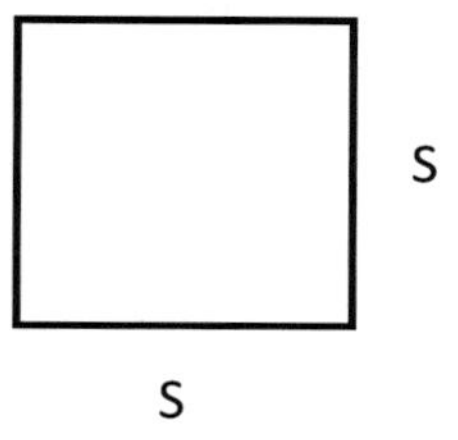

Rectangles

Area = L x W

Perimeter = 2L + 2W

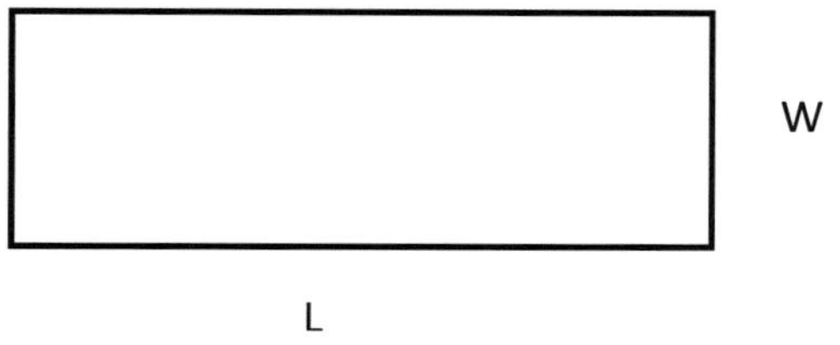

Parallelogram

Area = base x height

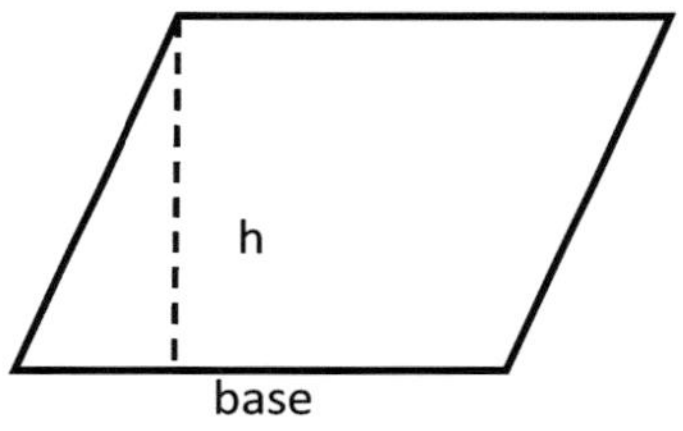

Trapezoid

Area = ½(base1 +base2) x height

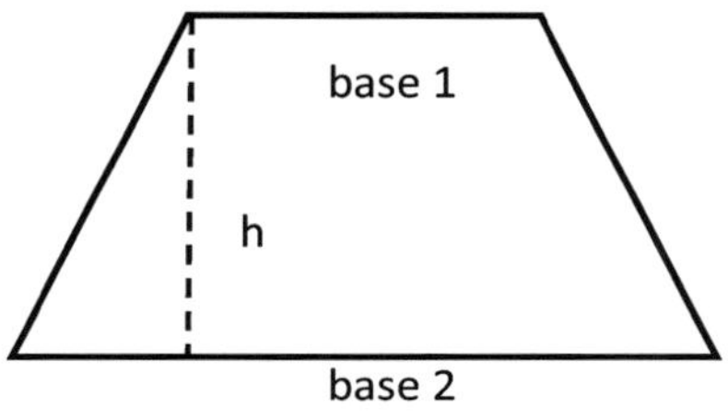

Angle Measures

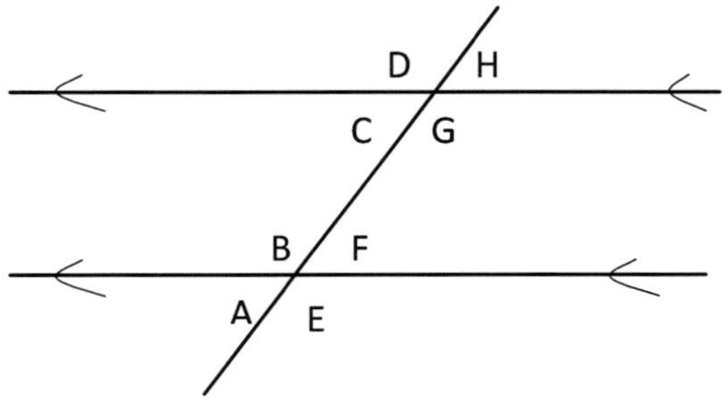

When a line crosses two parallel lines several rules apply:

Corresponding angles are congruent:

$\angle A = \angle C \quad \angle B = \angle D \quad \angle E = \angle G \quad \angle F = \angle H$

Alternate exterior and alternate interior are congruent:

$\angle A = \angle H \quad \angle B = \angle G \quad \angle E = \angle D \quad \angle F = \angle C$

Straight lines add to 180˚:

$\angle A + \angle B = 180° \quad \angle G + H = 180°$ *... etc.*

For any lines that cross, the angles across from each other are congruent, a concept called "vertical angles":

$\angle A = \angle F \quad \angle B = \angle E \quad \angle C = \angle H \quad \angle D = \angle G$

For any geometric shape, the total number of degrees in the interior of the shape = (n-2) x 180˚ where n = the number of corners in the shape

Example: A triangle has 3 corners and (3-2) x 180˚ = 180˚ total

A square, rectangle, or parallelogram has 4 corners and (4-2) x 180˚ = 360˚ total

Lines

Slope Intercept Form: y=mx +b

where x and y are points on the line, m is the slope, and b is the y intercept

Slope = $\frac{y-y^1}{x-x_1}$

Parallel lines have the same slope

Perpendicular lines have negative reciprocal slopes

Example: Line A slope = 3/5, the perpendicular Line B would have a slope of -5/3

Distance formula: d= $\sqrt{(x-x^1)^2 + (y-y^1)^2}$

Example: Find the distance between (4,9) and (8,6)

d= $\sqrt{(4-8)^2 + (9-6)^2}$ = $\sqrt{25}$ = 5

Midpoint formula: Midpoint = $(\frac{x+x^1}{2}, \frac{y+y^1}{2})$

Example: Find the midpoint between (6,5) and (10,-1)

$\left(\frac{6+10}{2}, \frac{5+(-1)}{2}\right) = (8,2)$

Sequences and Combinations

Arithmetic Sequences – sequences by addition or subtraction. Example: 2, 4, 6, 8 or 18, 10, 2, -6

Geometric Sequences – sequences by multiplication or division. Example: 3, 9, 27 or 100, 50, 25

Basic Combinations – Sometimes the Math section asks how many ways a certain set of items can be arranged. For example, a student ID card has five digits, 0-9. If numbers can be used more than once, how many different student ID numbers are possible?

10x10x10x10x10 = 100,000 different ID numbers

If each number (0-9) can only be used once per ID card: 10x9x8x7x6 = 30,240 different numbers

Basically, you multiply the number of options you have for each spot. In the first example, there are 10 options (0, 1, 2,...9) for each of the five spots. In the second example, each time you use a number it is no longer an option anymore, so you multiply by one less each time.

Advanced Algebra and Definitions

$X^3(X^2) = X^5$	$(X^3)^3 = X^9$	$2X^3 + X^3 = 3X^3$	$4X^6(8X^2) = 32X^8$
Add the exponents	Multiply the exponents	Combine like terms	Multiply terms, add exponents

For problems involving f(x), g(x), etc., you usually need to do some kind of substitution.

Example: $F(x) = x^2 + 3$ $\quad F(2) = 2^2 + 3 = 7$ $\quad F(x+h) = (x+h)^2 + 3$

Rational Numbers – Any integer, fraction, terminating decimal, or repeating decimal. The opposite are Irrational Numbers which neither terminate nor repeat. They go on forever with no pattern (example is π).

Real Numbers – All rational and irrational numbers

Integers – ...-4,-3,-2,-1, 0, 1, 2, 3, 4...

Whole Numbers – 0, 1, 2, 3, 4, 5...

Prime Numbers – Numbers that can only be divided evenly by 1 and themselves

Examples: 2, 13, 29

Further Reading for those Looking to Score Above 30

A few more advanced concepts occasionally show up near the end of the test. I will not give these formulas due to their complexity and because they all together show up only about two to five times per test. Search for the following concepts online or in a math book if you are interested in learning them. You do not have to know them in depth – the basics will do. Many of the following formulas are included in my calculator programs available at *www.ACTCalculatorFormulas.com.*

Imaginary Numbers: know what i, i^2, i^3, and i^4 equal; how to simplify exponents larger than i^4

Logarithms: the basic identities of a logarithm; the change of base formula

Multiple Variables: the substitution method and/or the elimination method

Trigonometric Graphs: define the period and amplitude and be familiar with the basic shape

Trig Functions: know which function(s) are positive and negative in each quadrant (the "All Students Take Calculus" trick); know how to get inverses on your calculator ($\sin^{-1}, \cos^{-1}, \tan^{-1}$); know how to use SOHCAHTOA within a coordinate plane.

Volume Formulas: cube and cylinder

Note: *these formulas are easier than they sound, but they are not all that important. I don't recommend learning them unless you have previously worked with them in a math class.*

The Basic Tips

1. *Your Calculator is Your Friend*

The calculator is a powerful tool for the ACT Math Test. In addition to its use for basic mathematical functions, it can solve difficult problems more quickly than through longhand formulas. Perhaps most importantly, it can be used to figure out problems you otherwise may not know. Here are two examples:

Bill has decided to get in shape for the upcoming football season. He decided to do 25 sit ups today (day 1) and 10 additional each day for the next month. How many sit ups will Bill do over the 30 day month? **Difficulty: 2**

A. 4160
B. 4750
C. 5100
D. 5350
E. 7325

The correct answer is C. I immediately start punching numbers in my calculator when I see a problem like this one. As long as you can keep count of how many numbers you have punched in, you can easily finish a problem like this in a minute or two. Time yourself and I bet you are surprised how fast your calculator can perform long problems such as this.

Note: The formula for the "sum of an arithmetic series" could also be used to complete this problem. This formula is not included in my formula sheet because of its complexity (and your calculator can do the job anyway).

A more advanced example of using your calculator to solve a problem you otherwise may not know:

For $0 < x < 2\pi$, if $\sin x < 0$ and $\cos x > 0$, what are the possible values of x? **Difficulty: 5**

A. $x = 2\pi$ or π
B. $\frac{3\pi}{2} < x < 2\pi$
C. $\pi < x < \frac{3\pi}{2}$
D. $\frac{\pi}{2} < x < \pi$
E. $0 < x < \frac{\pi}{2}$

The correct answer is B. Here's a relatively easy approach to solving this problem with your TI calculator:

Step 1 – Press "Mode" then choose "Radians" (you are working with radians here, not degree measures).

Step 2 – Begin to test values. So if you were testing answer E, you would find the sin and cos of a value between 0 and π/2. I would probably use π/4 as the test value. As another option, you could enter π/2 in your calculator, find that it equals 1.57, and use any value between 0 and 1.57 as your test value.

Next, you would enter sin(π/4) into your calculator (or whatever test value you chose), finding it equals .71. Choice E would now be disqualified because the sin is positive (the directions say sin must be < 0). Following this testing process for each answer choice, you will eventually find that only a value between 3π/2 and 2π gives you a negative sin and positive cos, which is what the problem asks for.

Note: Remember that your calculator is now in radian mode. You may need to change it back to degree mode for problems involving degree measures.

Note 2: The "All Students Take Calculus" trick would be the easiest way to solve the preceding problem. Search for "All Students Take Calculus" on Wikipedia.org if you are interested in learning the trick (it's quite simple), although it is not used often on the ACT.

2. *Find a Formula that Works*

Most questions, even the hardest ones, will fit into a basic mathematical formula (most of which are included in my formulas section). ACT will not surprise you with a question about Calculus. As the test goes on and the questions get more difficult, the concepts still remain the same for the most part. What is getting harder is the logic to find the right formula. So don't assume a problem is too difficult for you. **Think "What formula(s) could apply here?" or "How could I get the information I need?"** and you may be led to the solution. Here is an extended example:

A 5 inch by 12 inch rectangle is inscribed in a circle as shown below. Which is closest to the area of the circle in square inches? **Difficulty: 5**

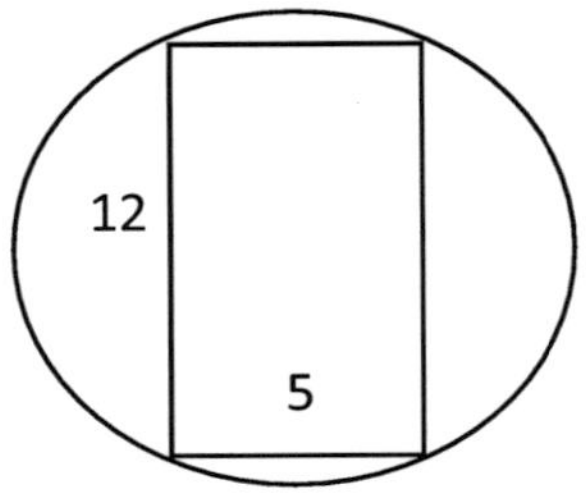

A. 12π
B. 34π
C. 42π
D. 63π
E. 165π

The correct answer is C. This problem seems difficult, but it can be solved with some simple concepts. **First, think about what information you will need. In this case, you want the area of the circle (Area = πr^2), so you will need to find the radius.** Now look at the information given to you. Math Test questions usually do not contain much unnecessary information, so chances are you will need to work with the given rectangle. Now the one tricky part – by drawing a diagonal on the rectangle you form a diameter, which is equal to twice the radius (see figure below).

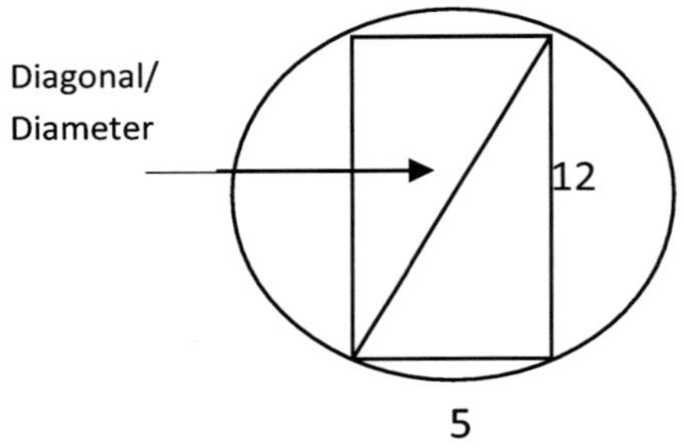

Since adding the diagonal created a right triangle, we can find the length of the diameter by simply using the Pythagorean Theory:

$a^2 + b^2 = c^2$

$5^2 + 12^2 = \text{diameter}^2$

$\text{diameter}^2 = 169$, diameter = 13

radius = .5(13) = 6.5

area = $\pi r^2 = \pi 6.5^2 = 42.25\pi$ (C, 42π, is closest)

We just did a very difficult ACT problem using only the Pythagorean Theory and the area of a circle formula. Find the formula that makes sense for the situation; chances are the math is easier than you think!

Note: *This problem is a great example of another little trick. Say this problem just plain stumps you. You still want to make as educated a guess as possible. Find the information you know and use it! Maybe you remember the formula for the area of a rectangle, area = length x width. So, the area of the rectangle equals 60. In my opinion, the circle looks to be about twice as big as the rectangle. So I will guess the area of the circle is about 2 x 60 = 120 square units. Next, I test the answers and see which numbers are near my educated guess. Choice C gives us 42 x π, which equals 131.95 – pretty close to my guess of 120. This answer seems to make sense. Choice B, which equals 106.81, would be a fair option as well. The other choices are way too high or low and should not be considered.* ***The main point: If possible, use logic and your calculator to narrow down choices and make a more accurate guess.***

3. *Use Dummy Numbers to Make Problems Easier*

Most students agree that it is easier to work with actual numbers than with variables. By using "dummy numbers" you can turn a problem involving variables into one with regular numbers. You can use dummy numbers on most problems involving simplification, on any problem that says something like "if x is any integer", and in a few other assorted situations. I will illustrate dummy numbers through a simple example.

The expression $4(x + 9) - 2(3x - 6)$ equals: **Difficulty: 1**

A. $-x + 24$
B. $x + 30$
C. $-2x + 30$
D. $-2x + 40$
E. $-2x + 48$

The correct answer is E. This problem is fairly easy to complete algebraically, but it will also serve as a basic example of using "dummies". Using dummies is quite easy. You simply make x any number, complete the problem, and find which answer matches up. You want to use a small number for ease, but avoid using 1 as your dummy.

So I'll say x=2. Now the given equation = $4(2 + 9) - 2(3(2) - 6) = 44$.
Next, I carry the dummy to the answers. Substituting x=2 in each answer choice shows that when x=2, Choice E also equals 44. Since when x=2 both equations equal 44, Choice E must be correct. A more difficult example using dummy numbers is found in Sample Problem 9.

Note: "Dummies" can be used in many situations, but not all the time. In some problems they simply will not make sense. As you go through practice tests, pay attention to which situations work for dummies and which do not.

4. *Draw! Plot! Test! Write the Info and Find an X!*

Struggling with a problem? Try one of these tips to get going in the right direction:

a. *Draw*

Here's a tip you have heard from math teachers for years. Draw diagrams whenever you can. It always helps to visualize a problem, especially when working with word problems.

b. *Plot*

For problems involving equations of lines or basic X and Y axis graphs, manually plotting lines and/or points can help to clarify a problem or at least narrow down the possibilities. Additionally, you can use the "Y=" button on your graphing calculator to plot more complex graphs.

c. *Test*

Test answer choices to see if they fit in the problem ("working backwards"). Eliminate answer choices that do not seem to make sense. Use your calculator and be creative; different problems present different ways to test values. Sometimes working backwards is faster and more accurate than doing a problem the conventional way!

d. *Write the Info and Find an X*

Start the problem by writing out all the mathematical information you are given. Then establish exactly what you are looking for; this will be your "X" variable (or Y or Z or whatever you want to call it). Now try to find a bridge from the information you are given to the value of your X variable. The bridge will usually be some kind of formula. Check out Sample Problem 1 on the following page for an example that clarifies this concept.

Sample Problems

1. The distance of a line is 10 units. One end of the line is at (9,2) and the other end has an X coordinate of 1. Which value could be the Y coordinate of this other end? **Difficulty: 3**

   A. 6
   B. -2
   C. 8
   D. 10
   E. -6

The correct answer is C. This problem is an example of how you need to be able to work with formulas multiple ways.

Given: Distance = 10, point one = (9,2), point two = (1,y)

$$d = \sqrt{(x - x^1)^2 + (y - y^1)^2}$$

$$10 = \sqrt{(9 - 1)^2 + (2 - y)^2}$$

square both sides to get $100 = 64 + (2 - y)^2$

$36 = (2 - y)^2$, Choice C (y=8) is the only answer that makes this true

Note: Notice how the first thing I do is neatly write out the information I am given. I also establish a variable to define the value I am looking for (this is the "y" in point two). Next I find the "bridge" to the answer, which happens to be the distance formula in this case. From there, it is just a matter of completing the algebra.

2. What is $\frac{8x}{5} - \frac{2y}{3}$ equal to? **Difficulty** = **2**

   A. $\frac{14xy}{15}$
   B. $\frac{24x-10y}{15}$
   C. $\frac{8x-4y}{5}$
   D. $\frac{8x-2y}{2}$
   E. $\frac{15x-6y}{5}$

The correct answer is B. This problem is about finding a common denominator and knowing basic rules about fraction subtraction. I demonstrate below.

$\frac{8x}{5}\left(\frac{3}{3}\right) = \frac{24x}{15}$, $\frac{2y}{3}\left(\frac{5}{5}\right) = \frac{10y}{15}$, $\frac{24x}{15} - \frac{10y}{15} = \frac{24x-10y}{15}$

3. Bill has an average of 82 through his first 5 tests in history. What score must he achieve on his 6th test to bring his average to an 84 for the term (all tests are out of 100 points)? **Difficulty : 4**

   A. 80
   B. 86
   C. 90
   D. 94
   E. 98

The correct answer is D. ACT loves this question and you definitely may see something similar on the test. This question mainly deals with the definition of an average.

First of all, I like to think of an 82 average as meaning he got an 82 on every single test. This simplifies things and, of course, 5 scores of 82 would equal an 82 average.

Average = $\frac{Total\ Points}{\#\ of\ trials}$

His current average of 82 over 5 tests means he has 410 total points $(82 = \frac{410}{5})$

To average an 84 over 6 tests he would need 84 x 6 = 504 total points $(84 = \frac{504}{6})$

To go from his current 410 points to 504 points he needs a 94 on the next test (504 – 410 = 94)

4. Bill just got hired as a sales agent for a local baseball team. Bill receives a base salary of \$20,000 plus \$.25 for each ticket he sells through phone calls and \$.40 for each ticket he sells through online advertising. If x represents the number of phone sales Bill makes this season, and y represents the number of sales he generates through online advertising, which equation models Bill's overall salary for the year (all units are in dollars)? **Difficulty: 1**

   A. xy(20,000 + .25 + .40)
   B. 20,000 + .25x + .40y
   C. 20,000x + .65y
   D. .25y + .40x
   E. 20,000 – .25x – .40y

The correct answer is B. 20,000 is Bill's salary without any sales, so that does not depend on any variable. .25x represents the $.25 extra he gets each time he sells a ticket over the phone. .40y represents the $.40 he gets for each online sale. All these added together will make up his overall salary for the year.

Note: If you have a tough time with word problems, underline the mathematical information in the problem and figure out exactly what the question is asking. Now use the tip "Write the Info and Find an X" (page 36) to get through the problem

5. In the right triangle below, what is the value of (sin A)(tan B)? **Difficulty: 4**

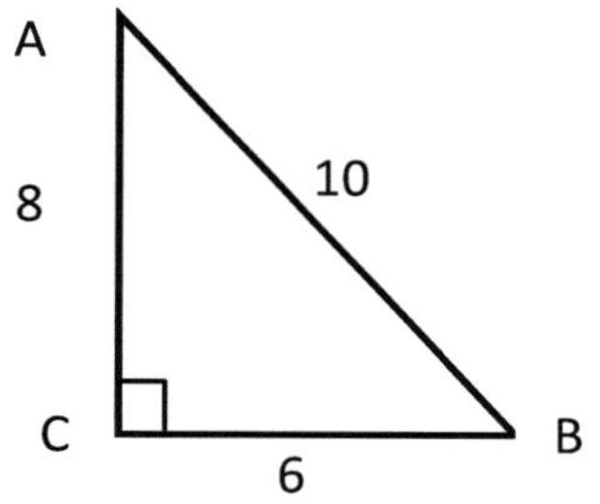

A. 16/15
B. 1
C. 4/5
D. 3/5
E. 4/15

The correct answer is C. This question combines SOHCAHTOA, multiplication, and basic fraction reduction. **It helps to know SOHCAHTOA well; you use it two to four times per test.**

$\sin A = \frac{Opposite}{Hypotenuse} = \frac{6}{10}$ $\tan B = \frac{Opposite}{Adjacent} = \frac{8}{6}$

$(\sin A)(\tan B) = \frac{6}{10}\left(\frac{8}{6}\right) = \frac{48}{60}$ $\frac{48}{60} = .8 = \frac{4}{5}$

Note: You can reduce the fraction using common factors, or you can get a decimal and then press "Math" then "Frac" (Option 1) on your TI calculator to get the reduced fraction.

6. Jim's skateboard ramps are built on level ground and slope upward at 20%, which means the ramp rises 20 feet vertically for each 100 horizontal feet. If Jim builds a ramp that rises 6 feet vertically, how long is the ramp in horizontal distance? **Difficulty: 3**

   A. 12 feet
   B. 24 feet
   C. 30 feet
   D. 36 feet
   E. 42 feet

The correct answer is C. This problem can look difficult, but it actually is a fairly basic ratio problem. In fact, **you will use ratios to solve about three to five problems on the ACT. Don't forget about them!** See the explanation below for clarification on using ratios.

The ramps rise 20 feet vertically for each 100 horizontally = $\frac{20\ vertical\ feet}{100\ horizontal\ feet}$

This ramp rises 6 feet vertically for each x feet horizontally = $\frac{6\ vertical\ feet}{X\ horizontal\ feet}$

We know they both follow the same 20% slope, so they can be compared in a ratio

$\frac{20}{100} = \frac{6}{X}$, Now you cross multiply to get: $20x = 600$, $x = 30$ feet

7. If $15x = 9(x-4)$, then x =? **Difficulty: 1**

   A. 6
   B. $3\ \frac{2}{3}$
   C. $-4\ \frac{3}{15}$
   D. -6
   E. -15

The correct answer is D. This is a basic algebra problem. I'll break it down step by step.

First distribute the 9: $15x = 9x - 36$

Now subtract 9x from both sides: $6x = -36$

Divide both sides by 6: $x = -6$

8. Which of the following could be the equation for the graph in the standard (x,y) coordinate plane below? (the sets of points on the graph are found on the curve) **Difficulty: 5**

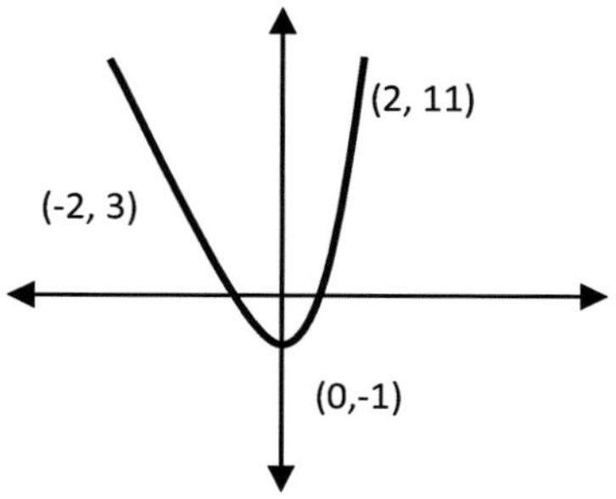

A. $y = x^2 + 2x + 3$
B. $y = 2x + 3$
C. $y = 2x^2 + 3x - 1$
D. $y = x^2 - 2x - 1$
E. $y = 2x^2 + 2x - 1$

The correct answer is E. You do not need to know anything about the graph of a parabola to complete this question. You just have to remember that each set of points has to fit in the equation. To demonstrate using the incorrect choice D:

I will first test to see if the point (0, -1) is on the curve: $y = x^2 - 2x - 1$
$x = 0, y = -1$; $-1 = 0^2 - 2(0) - 1$; True, (0, -1) is a point on this curve

Now to test if (2, 11) is a point on the curve: $y = x^2 - 2x - 1$
$x = 2, y = 11$; $11 = 2^2 - 2(2) - 1$; False, (2,11) is not a point on this curve

So (2, 11) is not a point on the graph of $y = x^2 - 2x - 1$ – Choice D can't be correct
Now try to test each point in the equation for choice E; you will find that they all work

Note: You can view graphs and test points easily using the "Y=" button and the "Trace" button on your TI calculator, although working by hand usually is faster.

9. If a and b are any positive integers, what value(s) of x, if any, will make $|ax - b| = |bx - a|$? **Difficulty: 6**

A. 1 , -1
B. 2
C. $\frac{a-b}{b-a}$
D. all real integers
E. no real integers

The correct answer is A. First of all, you have to know the definition of "absolute value" to complete this problem (if you don't know it, look it up). We will use dummy numbers to make this problem much easier:

a and b can be any positive integer, so I will use a = 2 and b = 3. Now the problem looks like:
$|2x - 3| = |3x - 2|$

It is difficult to do algebra when two absolute values are involved, so I will work backwards and see which answer fits.

Choice A: x = 1 $|2(1) - 3| = |3(1) - 2|$ True ; x = -1 $|2(-1) - 3| = |3(-1) - 2|$ True

Thus, Choice A works. At this point you could eliminate every other choice except for D. -1 and 1 are real integers, so Choice D could still possibly be correct. Now I will test a new x value to see if D is correct.

x=5 $|2(5) - 3| = |3(5) - 2|$
False. Since x=5 does not make this expression true, "all real integers" cannot be the value of x, and Choice A is confirmed as the right answer.

Note: You will get the same results if you use a= 8 and b = 35 as your dummies. The directions said only that a and b are positive integers, so any numbers will work.

10. In the figure below, lines p and q are parallel. What is the measure of angle x?
Difficulty: 3

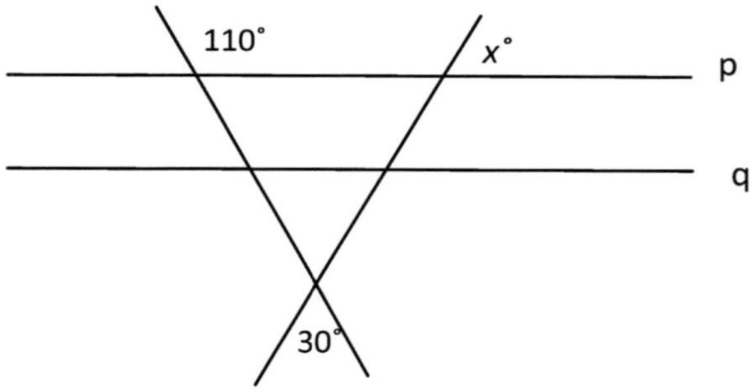

A. 30°
B. 110°
C. 70°
D. 100°
E. 80°

The correct answer is E. This problem is a good review of several angle measure properties. In problems such as this (and really any problem), you want to **fill in any information you know**.

Taking it step by step:
First, because straight lines add to 180˚, I write in 70˚ under the given 110˚ measure
Next, because of the property of vertical angles, I write 30˚ across from the given 30˚ measure.

Now the diagram looks like this:

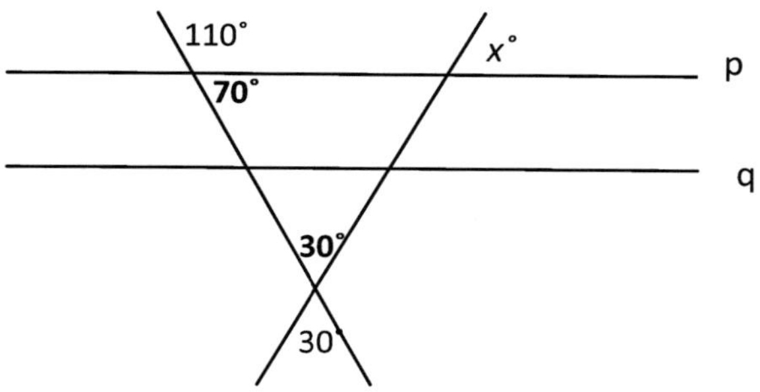

Since p and q are parallel, the 110˚ and 70˚ angles can be carried down (corresponding angles are congruent)
Now you can complete the 180˚ triangle as well (70 + 30 + 80 = 180)

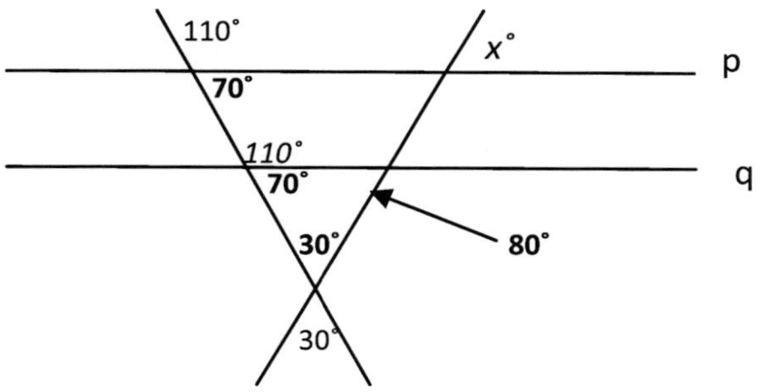

Now using the same properties I already used (vertical angles, lines adding to 180˚, and/or corresponding angles) you will find that x = 80˚. You could also use the property of alternate exterior angles to solve the problem at this point.

11. For the functions $f(x) = x^2 - 7$ and $g(x) = 3x + 4$, what is the value of $f(g(x))$? **Difficulty: 4**

A. $9x^2 - 3$
B. $x^2 - 3x - 3$
C. $9x^2 + 24x + 9$
D. $x^2 + 9x + 9$
E. $3x - 3$

The correct answer is C. This problem involves substitution and basic FOIL skills.

The key to these questions is to substitute the entire expression for x. To demonstrate:

$f(g(x)) = (3x + 4)^2 - 7$ **Notice how I square the entire expression
$f(g(x)) = 9x^2 + 12x + 12x + 16 - 7$
$f(g(x)) = 9x^2 + 24x - 9$

Whenever you see a problem with f(x), g(x), h(x), etc. just substitute whatever is inside the parenthesis for the x in the expression.

Two more examples using the functions above:

$f(4) = 4^2 - 7 = 9$ $g(x+2) = 3(x+2) + 4 = 3x + 10$

12. Reba is making a sandwich. She has 4 different kinds of cheese, 3 types of bread, and 5 different dressings. If each sandwich contains one type of cheese, one type of bread, and one dressing, how many different sandwiches could Reba make? **Difficulty: 3**

A. 60
B. 124
C. 12
D. 24
E. 256

The correct answer is A. This question follows the rule of basic combinations.

The rule is to multiply the number of options you have for each spot in the combination.

4 kinds of cheese x 3 types of bread x 5 different dressings

4 x 3 x 5 = 60 different sandwiches

Notes - Math

Notes - Math

Chapter 3 – Reading

Read through this chapter and then take an entire Reading practice test. Use a watch and write down how long it takes you to complete each passage of the practice test. After doing this, go back through this chapter and use the tips to form a general strategy.

Format and Basic Strategy

The third section of the ACT is Reading. You are given 35 minutes to read four passages and complete 40 questions testing your comprehension. The questions are not in any order based on difficulty.

The four passages always have the same headings. The first passage is Prose Fiction, the second is Social Science, the third is Humanities, and the fourth is Natural Science. When you receive your ACT score report, the Prose Fiction and Humanities will be grouped under the heading Arts/Literature, and the Sciences will be grouped under the heading Social Studies/ Sciences. These two scores are added together then scaled to form your overall ACT Reading score.

The Reading Test is different from the others in that people can take very different approaches to the test and still finish with identical scores. Because of this, I start with a section detailing different strategies that successful students have used on this test. Many students struggle to complete this section on time, so some strategies focus particularly on time management. Find a couple of strategies that seem to work for you and experiment with them on practice tests. The general tips and tricks follow the strategy section.

Note: Read through all the strategies even if they do not apply to you. The concepts behind them will be helpful.

Strategies

1. *Save the Worst for Last*

It is always beneficial to do the passage that is hardest for you last. In this case, if you run out of time you will have already completed your best passages. The two passages that give students the most problems are Prose Fiction and Natural Science. The other passages usually are a bit easier than these two. Take practice tests to determine which passage tends to be the hardest for you.

Some students find Natural Science the most difficult because it usually contains the toughest vocabulary and most confusing language. Natural Science already is the last passage, so you do not need to change the order if it is the most difficult for you.

Prose Fiction is different than the other passages in that you are working with a story instead of facts. If you find interpreting the story to be more difficult or time consuming than the other passages, then do Prose Fiction last. **Overall, about 50% of my students choose to do the Prose Fiction passage last**. Again, take practice tests to determine which passage is most difficult for you. If you choose to do Prose Fiction last, you will start with Passage 2 (Social Sciences) and then come back to Passage 1 after you have finished Passages 2, 3, and 4.

Generally, you want to decide which passage to complete last before test time; this way you are completely prepared. Conversely, a small percentage of my students choose to decide on their last passage during the test. They begin the test by quickly glancing at all four passages, finding which one looks the most difficult, and then marking that one to be completed last. Make sure you can do this quickly and effectively before employing this strategy. Otherwise it can be a waste of time.

Note: Each of the four Reading passages has exactly 10 questions, which makes it particularly simple to change the order in which you complete them.

2. *Taking it Straight*

If you have absolutely no issues completing the Reading Test in the given 35 minutes, you do not need to "save the worst for last". Simply take the test in its given order, reading each passage prior to answering the questions. This gives you 8 minutes and 45 seconds to complete each passage; not an easy task, but it certainly can be done.

3. *When Not to Read*

Some students have a hard time understanding certain passages. For example, maybe you are not a scientific person, and the Social Science and Natural Science passages just do not make a lot of sense to you. In this case, don't waste time reading these passages. Go directly to the questions and save time for searching back and finding answers. However, I recommend that you at least glance at the passage first to see if you can make sense of it. If you are sure that reading the passage will not help you, then you can go right to the questions. Reading each passage is generally the best option, but I have seen students bring scores up slightly by not reading certain passages.

Note: Practice and know which sections you will read and which you may not.

4. *The 10-10-10-5 and Related Strategies*

This is a great strategy for people who struggle to complete the Reading Test on time (which constitutes at least 50% of students from my experience). First, determine which section you will do last. Use the tips under Strategy 1 (page 48) to figure this out. Next, determine how long it takes you to complete a passage. Grab a clock and write down your times on a few practice passages. You want to take them comfortably, but don't act like you have unlimited time. Even if you struggle with time, a solid, attainable goal is ten minutes per passage.

Now "10-10-10-5" is pretty self-explanatory. Spend roughly ten minutes on each of your stronger passages, then five on your weakest. You don't need to watch the clock on every passage, but try to get comfortable finishing in the nine to eleven minute range. Even if you take eleven minutes on each of your first three passages, you will still have two minutes to make guesses on the final passage. Don't worry if you completely bomb one passage as long as you worked hard on the other three. **You can get 10 questions wrong and still finish with a 26 – 28 in Reading.** Strategies like this are why Reading is probably the most important test to practice. You want to have a plan coming into the test.

But how do you approach the final passage when you only have two to six minutes to complete it? My next strategy gives two options that will allow you to get some correct answers even with very limited time.

5. *Running Out of Time Strategy – When you have 2 – 6 minutes to complete a passage*

   a. *The Skim and Go*

      Depending on the amount of time you have remaining, either skim or read the passage. Now get down to business on the questions. Do them quickly without looking back to the text (you can look back a little if you have the time). This strategy works best for people who are good readers and can get a descent understanding of the passage quickly. If you choose this option, Tip 2, *Stick to the Main Idea*, will be essential to completing questions accurately in limited time (see page 51).

   b. *Line Numbers First*

      This is a popular strategy many of my students use when time is running short. When you reach the final passage, skip the text and go directly to the questions. Start by looking for any question that mentions particular line numbers. For example, these questions may say something like, "Based on the quote in lines 40 – 43..." or "The word in line 12..." Typically these questions can be answered only by looking at a small portion of the passage. Thus, they can be completed quickly without having to do much reading. If you still have time after completing these questions, begin on the others. Hopefully you will have some understanding of the passage from working on the "line number" questions and will be able to grab a few more points before time expires. Of course, always remember to guess on the remaining questions when you are absolutely out of time.

   c. *The Blind Guess – This applies to every section of the ACT, not just Reading*

      I often get asked, "Which is the best letter to pick when guessing?" "Should I fill in all the same letters?" Frankly, it does not matter at all, a guess is a guess. There is no pattern to the ACT answers; whether you guess the same letter or you guess all different letters, your chances of getting lucky remain the same. The main goal is to get your guesses filled in as quickly as possible.

The Basic Tips

1. *Read Through the Passage Quickly*

When initially reading a passage, you do not need to focus on every single detail. You want to read it like a magazine, not like a textbook. If a question does address a minor detail, you probably will have to look back to the text to find the answer anyway.

The goal is to find a few different aspects of the passage. **Most importantly, you want to find the main idea or argument of the essay. Second, you want to get a feel for the tone of the essay. Third, you want to form an idea of the progression of the essay**, so when you go back to look for an answer, you know where to look. I will go over each of these in more detail in the next few tips.

2. *Stick to the Main Idea – The most important tip in this section!*

Finding the main idea of each passage will give a major clue to answering at least half of the Reading Test questions. At least three questions on the Prose Fiction passage and at least five on each of the three other passages will directly relate to the passage's main point. This is not to say that ACT will ask "What is the main idea of this passage?" 20 times per test. But even questions about small details will relate to the theme.

> For example, let's say the Natural Science passage focuses on the amazing ways the White Catfish has adapted to its physical environment (where it lives) over the last ten thousand years, and how these adaptations have helped the species thrive. Correct answers will relate to that main idea. Here is a sample question from that passage:
>
> One could infer from the passage that the average White Catfish has become slightly smaller over the last ten thousand years because:
>
> A. They have more competition for food.
> B. The smaller size helps them to navigate narrow channels.
> C. The larger ones are unable to avoid predators.
> D. There is overfishing of large "trophy" catfish

We cannot have a definite correct answer since there is no passage. However, based on the description I would be fairly sure B is correct. Why? **Choice B says the adaptation came in response to their physical environment, which directly connects to the theme of the**

passage. As you can see by the example, this concept is fairly simple, but it is extremely effective. **Always keep an eye out for the theme of a passage, and then use that knowledge as you complete the questions.**

Note: As an exercise, read a practice passage and write down its main idea or argument in a maximum of two sentences. Now try doing the questions with your sentence(s) right in front of you. Do this on a few passages. Eventually you will not need the sentences; focusing on the main idea will become automatic.

Note 2: If you are having trouble pinpointing the main idea, look to the first and last paragraphs of the essay. The writer often establishes the main idea early in the essay and revisits it in the conclusion.

3. *Stick to the Main Idea Part Two – Within the passage*

Sometimes ACT will ask questions about one specific paragraph or a certain person's opinion. Take the same focus on the main idea; just apply it on a smaller scale.

For example, say a passage focuses on the debate between more taxation for better schools and roads, or less taxation so Americans can save more money. Here is a short paragraph taken from the passage followed by a question that relates to it:

Some economists argue that income taxes are unfair to those who do not have children in public schools or regularly use the highway system. Bill Evans, a professor at Big State University says, "Advanced toll systems have created a way to shift burdens to those who utilize the asset in question, which should be the goal of most forms of taxation."....

Based on his quote, Bill Evans most likely would support:

A. Higher tax rates for people with children in public schools.
B. One tax rate for all people.
C. Tax breaks for large families.
D. An increase in the overall tax rate.

The correct answer is A. Bill Evans's quote is tough to understand, but we really do not need it at all. The first sentence of the paragraph says that we are hearing from people who think income taxes are unfair to a certain set of people. This is the main idea of the paragraph, and Choice A fits right in with this theme. Just as in the previous tip, **you want to keep in mind the bigger picture as you answer the question**. Also, as I will explain in Tip 5, don't limit yourself just to Bill Evans's quote (even though that is what the question mentions); read around it to obtain a better understanding.

4. *Tone Tells – The second most important tip in this section!*

The tone of a passage gives major clues to answers. The tone is the attitude of the author towards the subject of the passage. **When reading the text, try to get a feel for how the author approaches his subject.** For example: Is he taking a scientific approach to explaining it? Is he using a lot of metaphors and using a symbolic, artsy approach? Is she excited about the subject? Does the subject anger her? When doing practice problems, look for answer choices that fit with the tone of the author. For example, if an author consistently talks about his home country of India with respect and longing, it will be presented that way in the correct answer choice. If your answer conflicts with the tone of the author you probably want to reevaluate your choice.

For example, let's say a passage focuses on how dogs can help cure people who suffer from depression. Let's say the author takes a scientific tone to explain this phenomenon, concentrating on the physical changes in the person's body due to the presence of a dog. You may see a question like this:

Dogs especially help to cure depressed senior citizens because:

A. Seniors often have few other companions besides the dog.
B. The dogs bring back memories of the senior's childhood pets.
C. Seniors usually have not had a pet for many years.
D. Seniors show increased serotonin levels in the presence of dogs.

The correct answer is D. I mentioned that the author took a scientific tone when explaining this phenomenon, and Choice D is the only one that matches this tone. You may want to group this tip with Tip 2, *Stick to the Main Idea.* The tone and the main idea usually go hand in hand.

In the Fiction section, it will also help to get an idea of the personality of the characters in the passage. Often ACT will try to trick you with questions about a character's disposition.

For example, in line 65 of a passage, Jean comes home from work and says, "I hate my job. Everyone who works there is a jerk." But in the rest of the story she gets along with her coworkers and is quite happy at work. You may see a question like the following.

One can infer from the quote in line 65 that Jane:

A. Is going to start looking for a new career.
B. Is upset about an event that happened at work that day.
C. Has coworkers who are disrespectful and mean.
D. Will become a rodeo clown.

The correct answer is B. If you only look at the quote you may expect A or C to be the answer. But you also have to know the character to determine the tone of the statement. I previously stated that Jane was happy at work, so the choice that makes the most sense is B. This was made easier since I told you directly that she liked her job. During the test it may not be that simple. You may have to look back in the text briefly to obtain an accurate picture of the character in question. This example also connects to my next tip.

5. *Don't Only Read the Lines They Mention*

Usually about two to four questions per passage will mention some line numbers. For example you would see "From the quote in lines 40-44…" or "The term 'passed over' as it is used in line 18 refers to…"

The key on these questions is: **Don't focus only on the line(s) mentioned in the question. Read around the mentioned lines and get some context for the part of the passage they are asking about.** In fact, sometimes the answer will be clearly stated right in the next line! A little extra reading on these questions will enhance your performance immensely.

6. *If it Sounds "A Little Wrong," it Probably is Wrong*

ACT tries to trick you by giving answer choices that are partly correct, but also contain a few words that really do not fit. These choices are tempting because they do have some truth to them. Be careful though! If even a small part of an answer is wrong, the whole answer will be wrong. Here is an excerpt from a passage and an example:

> Kyle saw Jim McCafrey, the carefree music shop owner, as an idol and mentor. Despite the fact that they had not talked in many years, Kyle was more excited and anxious to see Jim than any of his old friends. When Kyle was a teenager, McCafrey first showed him how to play the piano, instilling in him a deep appreciation for all types of music. Twenty years later Kyle was considered one of the greatest rock and roll pianists in the country. Kyle began to feel his nerves as he stepped into the music shop.

Which of the following most accurately describes the upcoming meeting between Kyle and Jim McCafrey?

A. Kyle is nervous about seeing Jim McCafrey because he is unsure whether he can live up to Jim's expectations.
B. Despite being nervous about an upcoming concert, Kyle is excited to see his old mentor Jim McCafrey.
C. Despite being a famous pianist, Kyle is overcome with emotion when it comes to meeting Jim McCafrey several years after their last contact.
D. Kyle is worried that Jim McCafrey might be upset because Kyle has not contacted him since becoming a famous musician.

The correct answer is C. All the other options contain some truth, but also contain a few words that are clearly wrong. Choice A says Kyle is unsure whether he can live up to Jim's expectations. This is incorrect because Kyle is a very well-regarded pianist and Jim is characterized as a carefree person. Choice B says Kyle is nervous about an upcoming concert, which is not found anywhere in the text. Choice D is wrong because nothing suggests that McCafrey is upset at Kyle. Choice C is the only 100% correct answer.

Note: Use this tip to eliminate choices quickly and improve your time. Of course, you need to be careful. You don't want to eliminate every single answer choice! Just look out for words that are <u>clearly incorrect</u> and avoid settling on partly right answers.

Note 2: Sometimes answer choices can be eliminated just because their wording does not fit with the tone of the essay (see Tip 4).

7. *Search Smart*

Many questions force you to look back into the text to find answers. Sometimes these answers are stated plainly in the text, and sometimes you need to interpret the passage a bit. Either way, the key is to find the needed information quickly, and then to understand it as best you can. Here are a few tips to improve your speed and skill when looking back through the text for answers:

a. *Don't Just Find Words, Understand Them*

A lot of times students find the part of the passage they are searching for, find text nearby that resembles an answer choice, and then choose that answer without thinking. If you have done this, ACT pulled one of their favorite tricks on you. **When you find the part of the passage you need to answer a question, stop, read, and think. You already are 75% of the way to the right answer; don't rush it now!** ACT always gives answer choices that look correct at first glance, but after a few seconds of reading, you find that they are wrong. Remember, don't just find words, understand them. Try the following example working backwards. Read the question first and then search back into the paragraph, just as if you were looking back during a test.

> My Aunt Margret, who never took to the farmer's life, ran an electronics store. Our small town was one of the few where TVs and video games were available to be bought locally. Children from neighboring towns always held us in a certain esteem due to this fact. Buses full of rival high school athletes, uniforms dirty, lined up after games to get the newest movie or CD. With no competition for hundreds of miles, Margret's store prospered for fifteen years.

> Children from neighboring towns admired residents of the narrator's town because:
>
> A. Aunt Margret lived there.
> B. Buses of high school athletes went to the town.
> C. It had the largest downtown business district.
> D. It was the only town in the area with an electronics store.

The correct answer is D (concentrate on the second and third sentences of the paragraph if you did not get it). You may be tempted to choose B because the "buses of athletes" are mentioned just after the sentence about the "children from neighboring towns," but that choice is there purely to trick you. ACT tries this same trick many times in every Reading Test; remember, don't just find words, understand them!

b. *Have an Idea of Where You Will Find the Answer*

After reading the passage, you should have some idea of the progression. The following is an example of the progression of a typical essay.

1st paragraph – Introduction – Is football surpassing baseball as "America's game"?

2nd – 4th paragraph – Facts about football's rising popularity

5th and 6th – Experts who believe football has surpassed baseball

7th and 8th – Facts saying baseball still is our favorite sport

9th – Expert opinion saying baseball is still on top

10th – Conclusion – It depends how you look at it

Let's say a question read "How much higher are television ratings for football games than for baseball games?" You would start by looking somewhere around the 2nd paragraph. If a question asked about baseball great Yogi Berra's opinion, you would probably look at the 9th paragraph. ACT passages are skillfully written and every one of them will be well organized. When going back to find an answer, try to remember the progression and use it to speed up your search.

Note: The standard organization for an ACT passage is that general introductory information is in the beginning, supporting details are in the middle, and big picture statements about the significance of the topic are near the end. Of course, every passage is different, but many follow this basic pattern.

c. *Helpers for Your Search*

When searching for answers, you want to look for words and punctuation that will catch your eye quickly. Some things that are easily noticed: capitalized proper nouns, unusually long words, quotation marks, and dates.

If possible, tailor your searches to looking for these easily noticed words. For example, if a question asks about stadiums in Norway, you would search for the word Norway (capitalized proper noun), not the word stadium. Or if the answer choices are all dates (1942, August 30, etc.) from the text, look for these before you look for anything in the question. Finding the dates will be faster than skimming for a few words from the question.

d. *Skim the Answers Prior to Searching*

It often helps to skim through the answer choices before you search back through the text (as opposed to just reading the question then searching). It will give you an idea of what you are looking for and speed up your search process.

e. *Underlining*

Some students like to underline anything they find important as they initially read through the text. Personally, I don't find this to be all that beneficial, but it does help some students slightly. If you think underlining could help your searching or your comprehension, give it a try on a practice test and see how it works for you.

Notes - Reading

Notes - Reading

Chapter 4 – Science

The final subtest, and perhaps the most feared, is Science. If you are not familiar with the Science Test, try at least two passages from a practice test before going through the "The Basic Tips" section.

Format and Basic Strategy

Science consists of seven passages with 40 total questions to be finished in 35 minutes. On the Science Test the questions go from easiest to hardest within each passage. So Passage One's fifth question will be harder than the first question of Passage One, but about the same difficulty as Passage Two's fifth question.

Science seems to be the section in which students are getting the worst advice, so be skeptical of strategies you hear about this test. If you think a strategy may work, try it on a practice test and see if it helps your score.

Before we begin I should mention that **the Science Test is not a test of your scientific knowledge.** Sorry, but an A+ in Biology is not going to put you at a big advantage. You are aware of this fact if you have taken a practice test. The Science Test is about reasoning and graph interpretation. Keep practicing and you will become familiar with the types of questions you will see on test day.

Note: Some students tend to over think this section, while others do not think enough. As you read through this section, try to determine which tips apply to you the most.

The Basic Tips

1. *Look Out for the Seven Question Passage*

Each Science Test consists of seven passages. Three of these are called "Data Representations," three are called "Research Summaries," and one is called "Conflicting Viewpoint". You can tell the difference easily because Data Representations have five questions per passage, Research Summaries have six questions, and the Conflicting Viewpoint has seven. The Conflicting Viewpoint is especially easy to spot because it typically has no pictures or graphs, just text that is divided into two conflicting opinions.

I recommend that students do the Conflicting Viewpoint (or "Seven Question Passage") last. When you see this passage, put a mark on your answer sheet, skip it, and go ahead. You can come back to it after you finish the rest of the passages.

Why do the Seven Question Passage last? Well, normally its questions take the longest to answer and are the most difficult overall. Science can be tough to finish in the allotted amount of time. If you do run out of time, it is better to be guessing on harder questions. Just be careful with your answer sheet. I immediately put a mark next to the number on my answer sheet as a reminder that I am skipping ahead.

Note: If you have absolutely no issues completing Science in the allotted time, you do not have to do the Seven Question Passage last. Just take the test in its given order.

2. *Don't Get Hung Up on the Hard Ones*

As I mentioned in this section's introduction, the first few questions on a passage can be considerably easier than the last few questions for that passage. Sometimes the last couple of questions on a passage can be very difficult, consume a lot of time, and in the end you may still get them wrong! **If you are puzzled by a question, circle it and move on. This will ensure you have time to complete all the easier questions.** Remember, every question, hard or easy, is worth the same amount of points. You may want to put a guess down on the questions you skip, and then change it if you have time to find the correct answer later. Don't leave anything blank!

Note: Pay attention to this tip and apply it as you take practice tests. Get comfortable with all of your strategies and you will be completely relaxed when it comes to test day.

3. *Don't Read*

Jump right into the questions without reading the text. It will save you time and not hurt your score at all. You can go back and read if it's necessary to answer a question, but do not start by reading the passage. I have not seen one student's score go down by using this tip, and I have seen many improve greatly from it.

4. *Look Where They Tell You to Look*

Every passage has several headings. Passages start with a short text which ACT refers to as "the passage" (I know, kind of confusing). Then you see other headings such as "Experiment 1," "Table 2," etc. Often questions say "From the results of Experiment 1..." or "Based on information presented in the passage..." When you see these statements go right to the mentioned section to find the answer. **That is, if it says "Based on Experiment 1...," look under the heading "Experiment 1" to find the answer.** 95% of the time the answer will be right where they tell you to look.

5. The *Progression from Chart to Passage*

The easiest way to solve most problems is by using the charts and graphs. However, on some problems you need to use information in the text. When you start a problem go to the chart first (go to whichever chart they mention in the question, or if none is mentioned, go to whichever one fits the question best). If the information you need is not found in the chart, then look in the description above the chart. If the information is not there, then look to the passage to find your answer. This may seem like a long process, but it should only take about ten to twenty seconds to get through it. As you practice more and study the rest of the tips this will become easy to do.

6. *Step by Step Method for Chart Questions*

The easiest questions in this section are those based directly off charts and graphs. If you are around the 16-20 range in Science, mastering this tip can raise your score to the low 20s right away. If Science is a strength for you, this tip will help you avoid mistakes and save time for more difficult questions.

Many different types of charts and graphs exist, but the basic strategy remains the same. I will demonstrate with a few examples based on the following two charts from the same passage. Go directly to the three practice questions before studying the charts, just as you would during the test.

Experiment 1 –

A 75 horsepower engine was submersed in a 65 degree Fahrenheit water tub and run at different speeds. After two minutes, the temperature was read in the tub.

Table 1	
Rotor speed (RPM)	Change in Temperature (degrees Fahrenheit)
1,000	1.1
3,000	2.4
5,000	5.1
7,000	10.4

Experiment 2 –

Several engines of different horsepower were submersed in the 65 degree Fahrenheit water tub; all were operating at the same rotor speed. The time was measured until the water reached 75 degrees.

Table 2	
Horsepower	Time elapsed (seconds)
65	138
75	124
85	112
95	102

Based on the results of Experiment 1, if the heat given off equaled 3.7 degrees, what would the rotor speed most likely equal?

A. 1000 RPM
B. 2000 RPM
C. 4000 RPM
D. 6000 RPM

The correct answer is C. This example may have been easy for you, but follow along anyway as I use it to present my technique for "chart questions".

Step 1: Go straight to the chart for Experiment 1. It is labeled Table 1.

Step 2: Find the information you are given and match it up to data in the table. **You generally match up information to the labels in the axes or headings of a chart.** Here we are given that the heat given off equals 3.7 degrees. In Table 1 we have a column whose unit is in degrees. Mark with your pencil where 3.7 degrees would fit in that column.

Step 3: Find out what value they are looking for and match that up to the given data. Again we match up using the axes and headings in the chart. Here they ask "What would the rotor speed equal?" We see in the chart that rotor speed is a column heading.

Step 4: Pull the information together. If heat released equals 3.7 degrees we must be somewhere between 3,000 and 5,000 RPM. Thus, C is the only answer choice that works.

Note: You will definitely see several questions similar to this on the ACT. The ACT often requires you to find values that are in between numbers on a chart, or that extend a chart further than its current scope. If you are unclear on this, no worries, you will see plenty of examples here and on practice tests.

Based on Experiment 2, as horsepower decreased, time elapsed:

A. Increased only.
B. Decreased only.
C. Increased, then decreased.
D. Decreased, then increased.

The correct answer is A. Fairly easy, but I'm sure some of you chose B and just realized you had it backwards. **Whenever you have a comparison like this, double check your answer to make sure you do not have it backwards.** It takes only a few seconds and it prevents the most common "stupid mistake" that students make on the entire ACT.

Based on Experiments 1 and 2, the rotor speed used for the motors in Experiment 2 was most likely:

A. 7000 RPM
B. 5000 RPM
C. 4000 RPM
D. 1000 RPM

The correct answer is A. This is a very difficult chart question that would surely be one of the last questions for this passage. We have to sort through two experiments, using information from each to find the answer. The trick is still to take it step by step, although the process is slightly different and the steps are more flexible because we are working with two experiments. **The main strategy here is to take one piece of information at a time and think through things step by step.**

Step 1: Figure out which value you are looking for, and then find similar values in the table. Here we want the rotor speed for Experiment 2. The only other place we see rotor speed is in the first column of Table 1. Chances are that you will need to use those values to answer the question; they don't expect you to make up a rotor speed from your own knowledge.

Step 2: Try to match up information from the two experiments. When two experiments are mentioned in one question, ACT wants you to find some kind of similarity between the two and carry the corresponding data from one chart to the other. You often will have to look in the description that precedes the table to find this similarity. For our example you may notice that a 75 horsepower engine was used in Experiment 1. We carry this information to Experiment 2 and find that when a 75 horsepower engine was used, the time to heat the water from 65 to 75 degrees was 124 seconds.

Step 3: Pull it all together. So we found it took 124 seconds to heat the water from 65 to 75 degrees with the 75 horsepower motor in Experiment 2. Back in Experiment 1, we see that they are measuring the change in temperature over two minutes (120 seconds), which matches up nicely to the 124 seconds we saw before **(keep an eye out for any similarities!)**. At 7000 RPM the temperature rose 10.4 degrees over the two minute trial period. So in both cases a 75 horsepower engine heated the water roughly 10 degrees over roughly two minutes. Thus, the engine was most likely at 7000 RPM in the second experiment.

OK, are you confused yet? This example is more difficult than 95% of ACT questions, so don't worry if you struggled with it. If you don't fully understand it, work through it slowly using my notes and pay special attention to places where I match information from chart to chart. **Carrying information from one chart to another is the key to solving problems that refer to multiple charts.**

7. *Don't be too Concerned with Extra Information*

Sometimes ACT gives you a bit of extra information that is unnecessary to solving the problem. If you come to a well thought out answer that does not incorporate some of the information in a question, go with it anyway. If your answer seems a bit shaky, see if it is possible to use the extra piece of information. There is no exact way to know which information in a question is unnecessary, but with a bit of thought you can usually figure it out. Here is an example:

> Scientists took two 85 horsepower engines similar to those used in Experiment 2. One was run at 7000 RPM and one was run at 3000 RPM. As compared to the 7000 RPM engine, the 3000 RPM engine let off:
>
> A. More heat.
> B. Less heat.
> C. The same amount of heat.
> D. There is no way of knowing.

The correct answer is B. The fact that we are using 85 horsepower motors is basically irrelevant. The question really asks, "What lets off more heat, a motor running at 7000 RPM or one at 3000 RPM?" You can get this answer from Table 1 or just from plain common sense!

Note: Often the extra piece of information will be right at the beginning of the question, as in the previous example.

This question leads to my next tip as well...

8. *Use Common Sense / Don't Shut Off Your Brain!*

Many times students get in the habit of frantically searching through the tables and text to find answers, completely forgetting to simply think about the question. All the ACT passages make sense scientifically. They will never trick you and say, for example, an ice cube is hotter than an oven. Use this to your advantage. I once had a very intelligent student spend five minutes arguing that a passage stated that flooding was more likely during periods of drought than heavy rain. Obviously he misinterpreted the text and was incorrect. He made an easy question very hard because he forgot to think. **Common sense and a bit of thought will make a world of difference on even the most difficult problems.**

9. *Work with the Numbers You are Given*

Here is a tip that can really help you narrow down your choices on certain problems. I'll explain it through a short example that again refers back to the tables printed earlier in this chapter.

Jim recreated Experiment 1 using the 75 horsepower engine, but now fitted it with a new radiator. At 3000 RPM the change in temperature would be:

A. Less than .5 degrees.
B. Between .5 and 2.4 degrees.
C. Between 2.4 and 5.1 degrees.
D. Greater than 10.4 degrees.

The correct answer is B, but C would be a fine choice as well. Why? At 3000 RPM the change in temperature in Experiment 1 is 2.4 degrees. Only Choices B and C contain the given number of 2.4 degrees. ACT only wants you to decide if the new radiator makes the change in temperature go up or go down. **ACT does not expect you to do advanced math or to accurately guess values in the Science section. Use the given numbers!**

Note: This tip also helps when you are completely clueless on a question. Always guess numbers that you see somewhere in the charts or passage; your chances of getting lucky will be much better.

10. *Skim the Answers First then Go to the Passage*

On questions with wordy answer choices, glance at the answers first before you look in the text or charts. If you know the choices, you know exactly what to look for in the text. Key words will jump out to you and you will save valuable time while solving the problem.

11. *Words are Almost Always Defined*

If you see a word in a question or chart that seems completely foreign to you, chances are that it is defined somewhere in the passage. The Science Test is not about vocabulary. The defined word usually will be in italics, which will make it easier to find. But only look for the definition if you truly need it to solve a problem! Otherwise you are just wasting valuable time.

12. *The Seven Question Passage*

OK, so you finished the rest of the test and you are ready for the Seven Question Passage. The Seven Question Passage <u>usually</u> is all text (no charts) and is divided into two conflicting viewpoints. The two people arguing are generally labeled “Scientist 1” and “Scientist 2” or “Student 1” and “Student 2”.

This passage is different from the others, so you have to approach it in a slightly different fashion. You still can go directly to the questions without reading, but when you go back to look for answers, you will have to do a fair amount of reading. Too much skimming on this passage can get you into trouble.

In fact, the Seven Question Passage can be similar to Reading Test passages in a few ways. Just as in the Reading section, you should try to understand the passage instead of just mindlessly searching for words that match answer choices. Furthermore, keep an eye out for the main idea or argument of this passage. **The main argument of the Seven Question Passage is usually the disagreement between the two scientists; if you can pinpoint the difference in their views you will have a major clue to answering about half of this passage's questions.**

Also, remember to use your common sense on this passage. If "Scientist 1" is arguing that global warming does not exist, all the questions about "Scientist 1" will support this opinion. You would not want to answer a question saying that "Scientist 1" says the earth's temperature has permanently risen 5 degrees, because this would conflict with his overall argument. If you think you have found an answer, but it conflicts with the scientist's main argument, go back and look it over.

Note: While this passage is certainly different than the others, it still shares many characteristics with the other Science passages. Don't hesitate to use other tips from this section on the Seven Question Passage.

Note: Occasionally the Seven Question Passage does contain charts. They will not be any different than the charts in the other passages. Approach them the same way that I mentioned earlier in this chapter.

13. *Real Science Questions*

The Science Test is much more about reasoning and interpreting graphs than actual science knowledge. However, once or twice per test ACT will throw you a legitimate science question. Here are a couple things to know for these questions:

a. *Three Terms to Know*

Independent variable – what you change in an experiment. For example, how much fertilizer you put on a plant.
Dependent variable – the result of the experiment. For example, how much each plant grows due to the different amounts of fertilizer.

Control – an untouched trial used for comparison. For example, this would be a plant with no fertilizer on it.

b. *Real Science Guesses*

If you are taking a guess on a "real" science question, go with terms that are not way out there. ACT expects you to know some science, but not rocket science. For example, you would guess the word "nucleus" instead of guessing "endoplasmic reticulum". Chances are ACT does not expect you to know the definition of "endoplasmic reticulum"!

Graphs and Common Concepts

I have gone over basic chart strategy with the tables above, but I would like to give a few pointers using graphs, as they can be just slightly different.

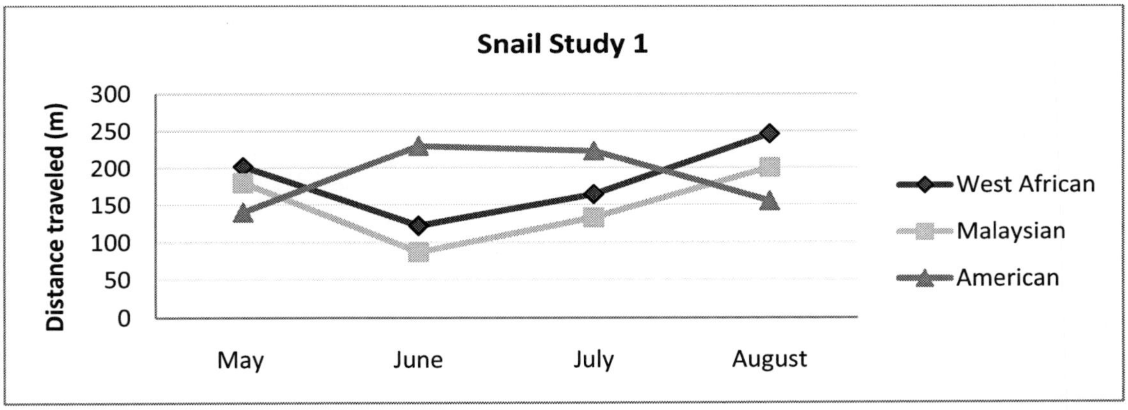

Figure 1

On any graph, the key to finding the needed data is to look at the axes. When you are "matching up" data from a question to a figure, you will find the key words you need on an axis. Here is an example:

The Australian snail moves approximately 154 meters in June. Which snail(s) is more active than the Australian in the same month?

A. West African and Malaysian
B. Malaysian and American
C. American only
D. All three snails are more active

The correct answer is C. The question gives us the month of June, which you can easily match up to the bottom axis. The question also gives us the number of 154 meters, which you can match up to the vertical axis. Now, draw a line across from each of these spots and actually plot where the Australian snail would be on the graph. Now it is very easy to solve this problem.

If you found this question easy, don't think this technique is not for you. This strategy will help you on even the most difficult of graphs and will improve your speed on the easier ones.

Note: Sometimes ACT will give you information that is off the chart. For example, a question might say that the Malaysian snail moves 250 meters in September. September is off the range of Figure 1, but <u>plot it anyway</u>. Make an educated guess of where the September point would be if the graph was continued. Your plotted point will be completely off the chart, but that is OK. Visualizing the question improves your chances of completing it correctly.

Note 2: There are countless different types of tables and graphs on the Science Test. Some can be quite strange looking and difficult to comprehend. If you do not understand a chart at first, don't hesitate to spend a little extra time trying to interpret it. Also look above the chart, as a description may clarify things. If you do not know what a chart is saying, it will be pretty tough to get the questions correct! And again, ***when in doubt, look to the axes for clues.***

A last word to those who still struggle to complete this section on time…

Practicing under timed conditions will sharpen your skills. Try taking 40 minutes for your first practice test, then 38 for the next, then 35 after you have some experience with this section. If you are running out of time, make sure you have finished all the easier questions. The best questions to make guesses on are the last few from the Seven Question Passage and, of course, any that puzzled you during the test. Finally, don't leave anything blank; you may get lucky!

Notes - Science

Notes - Science

Chapter 5 – Writing

After completing the four main sections of the ACT, you may also take the optional Writing Test. More and more colleges are requiring this test and, unless you see writing as a major weakness, it is probably to your advantage to give it a try. **Taking the Writing Test does not affect your composite score at all.** You receive an additional score on a 2 – 12 scale for the Writing Test, and you are given an additional Writing / English score which combines your Writing and English scores on a 1 – 36 scale. All your original subtest scores remain unchanged.

You probably have plenty of practice writing essays for your English and Social Studies classes, but writing under timed conditions is quite different. Pick a couple topics and write at least two timed practice essays before you take the test. Any issue that people disagree upon can be used as a practice topic.

Format and Basic Strategy

The Writing Test gives you 30 minutes to plan and write an essay. The topic or "prompt" is chosen by ACT and relates to some issue relevant to a high school student. You will not know the prompt until the test begins. Each prompt gives two options, for example: "Should high school be in session all year, or should a summer break be maintained?" It is your job to take a position on the issue and support your argument logically. ACT grades you on how well you write and how well you support your position.

This section contains several tricks and tips that all pertain to one goal: writing a well constructed ACT essay. I do not focus on general writing skills because you learn those in English class. I begin this section with a rundown of the exact standards ACT graders use when they score your essay. The tips and tricks follow.

Grading Standards

Your essay will be given a score of 1 – 6 by two separate graders. Their grades are combined to give you an overall score of 2 – 12 (12 is the best possible score). The following are the nine things you must do to get a top score on the ACT Writing Section. These are based on the exact standards ACT graders use when scoring your essay.

1. *Understand the Prompt*

    Your essay should directly address the prompt and stay focused on the topic. All your arguments should relate to the prompt in a straightforward fashion. Top-scoring essays show a clear understanding of the issue and encourage further intelligent discussion about it.

2. *Take a Position on the Issue*

    Each prompt gives two sides to an issue. Make sure you pick one side and stick with it for the entire essay. Be as persuasive as possible in supporting your position. Tip 2 gives a guideline for which side of the issue to pick.

3. *Evaluate Complications and Respond to Counterarguments*

    You should anticipate some of the arguments for the other side of the issue ("counterarguments") and respond to them briefly in your essay. This is elaborated on in Tip 5.

4. *Fully Develop Your Ideas*

    Concentrate on two or three main points and go into detail on each of them in your body paragraphs. Fully support your main ideas with several reasons and examples. Don't just write down a long list of undeveloped arguments. See Tip 4 for more on this.

5. *Organize and Sequence Your Ideas*

    Keep a basic organization pattern. Start with an introductory paragraph, then move on to a couple body paragraphs, and then finish with a concluding paragraph. Try to place all your arguments in a logical order that flows naturally. Figure out the sequencing of your essay before you start writing it (see Tip 1).

6. *Have a Clear Introduction and Conclusion*

An introduction and a conclusion are necessary parts of your ACT essay. See Tips 3 and 6 for extended sections on introductions and conclusions.

7. *Use Transitions*

Try to move from one idea to another smoothly and logically. An essay with no transitions appears choppy and will not earn a very high score. You want to begin thinking about transitions while initially planning your essay (see Tip 1).

8. *Vary Sentence Structure and Use Good Vocabulary*

This really comes down to your overall writing ability. Strong use of vocabulary looks great to ACT graders, but make sure the word truly fits in the sentence. Misuse of vocabulary will end up hurting your score.

9. *Avoid Errors*

No one wants to make mistakes in spelling or grammar, but it does happen. The main goal is to make sure the errors do not distract the reader from making sense of your essay. Go back and check for errors if you have some extra time after you finish the essay.

The Basic Tips

1. *Plan It Out!!!*

ACT puts an emphasis on having a well organized and logically sequenced essay. This is very difficult to accomplish if you do not take some time to plan. Your ACT booklet gives you a page to plan your work and you definitely should take advantage of it. I recommend using your first three to seven minutes to work solely on idea generation and general organization. Once you come up with a rough outline of your work, you will be able to write your essay quickly, and will easily make up for the time you spent prewriting. Everyone's writing style is different, but regardless you want to accomplish at least three things during the planning stage.

a. Conceive of a strong introduction and general thesis statement (one sentence that sums up your entire essay).
b. Come up with your basic arguments and make sure you can support them; find at least one response to a counterargument (argument for the other point of view).
c. Get an idea of the order of your essay and how you will transition between ideas.

After accomplishing these three tasks you will be ready to write a strong essay. Some of the tips below will elaborate on these ideas.

2. *Picking the Right Side*

In addition to testing your general writing skills, this section tests your ability to support an argument. So, **choose the side of the argument that you can support the best**. If the prompt asks "Should school be in session all year or should a summer break be maintained?" you may want to pick "school all year" even if the thought of it makes you cringe. If your best support for the summer break would be "I like to sit on the couch and watch baseball all day," this would not be the best choice. Don't worry; an ACT grader will not tell your friends that you want to be in school all year.

3. *Setting the Tone: Good Introductory Paragraphs*

Writing a great introductory paragraph is a difficult task, especially under timed conditions. For this reason, ACT graders do not expect an ultra-creative introduction. They mainly want you to accomplish a few basic tasks, which I list under the "Must Do's" heading on the next page. If you can effectively complete these four "must do's," you will be on pace for a solid score of 8 – 10, and an 11 or 12 will certainly be possible. Now, if inspiration strikes, a creative introductory paragraph can help you earn an extra point and/or put you on pace for a score of 11 or 12. I list some ideas for unique introductory paragraphs under the "Bonuses: Creative Openers" section on the next page.

Must Do's:

a. Make your introduction at least three sentences. You will probably lose a point if it is shorter than that. At the same time, **you don't want to repeat yourself or lose track of your arguments.** In fact, you want to avoid doing those things throughout your entire essay, not just in the introduction.

b. Speak to the topic of the essay and clearly present your view on the issue. You may want to come right out with your view in the first sentence, or you can wait a sentence or so if you are using a creative opening. Either way, your opinion on the issue should be distinctly stated fairly early in the paragraph.

c. Give some reference to the points you make in your essay. Try not to give away all your best supporting reasons, though. You may want to speak somewhat generally in the introduction and then get into the details of your main points later in the essay. As another tactic, you may want to give one example or detail that speaks to all your main points. Referencing your arguments makes for an easy but effective way to fill out your introductory paragraph.

d. Have one clear thesis statement. This sentence clearly presents your view on the issue. It should also either hint at your supporting arguments or just come right out with them. Many students like to simply end the introductory paragraph with an all-encompassing thesis sentence like:

> School should be extended to the summer months to keep teenagers out of trouble, prepare them better for college, and allow them more time to pursue non-required classes.

This kind of sentence does a good job of introducing your arguments and establishing your position, although something more creative will help slightly if you are shooting for a score of 11 or 12.

Bonuses: Creative Openers (Make sure you still follow all the "must do's"; they are needed whether you use a creative opener or not)

a. Tell an Anecdote (short story). Take your best example and relate it to the overall topic of your essay. Try to connect your story to as many of your arguments as possible. The story does not have to be 100% true, so meld it to fit your main points. Once you finish the anecdote, comment on it for a sentence or two, or go right into a thesis statement that plainly states your position and main arguments. Just don't ramble; starting with a long, slow-moving story will hurt your score.

b. Squash a significant counterargument. When skillfully done, this can make for an attention-grabbing start to an essay. Here is an example:

> Requiring children to stay in school during the summer seems to be an obvious way to improve young students' intellects and keep them focused on their studies. But in a world of diminishing attention sp ans, mandatory summer school would end up having the opposite effect....

You may go on to make the point that students would be too distracted and more dropouts would result. You still could tie in other unrelated points (like the need for summer jobs), especially if you use some smooth transitions.

c. Surprise the reader. Say something bold. Maybe start with an exclamation. Get creative. ACT readers read thousands of similar essays and appreciate some pizzazz. With that said, don't force it. A basic opening stating your view on the issue is superior to something creative that does not make sense and/or fit the topic. Here is an example of a surprising opening sentence:

> High school students are lazy. Their future jobs will not have summer breaks. Why should they get used to it as they prepare for adulthood?

The preceding sentence also demonstrates the tactic of starting with a rhetorical question (a question not intended to be answered). Rhetorical questions can be overused, so be careful, but sometimes they are a useful way to get your reader's attention.

d. Get historical. If you are familiar with the subject, you may be able to comment on the past and use it to support your future recommendations on the issue. Example:

> Summer breaks started because farm children were expected to help their parents over the summer months...

Note: Be careful when using creative openers. Misusing them will hurt your score. Basic, traditional introductory paragraphs can still earn high scores. Don't force it!

4. *Body Paragraphs: Supporting Your Arguments*

The ACT rewards fully-developed arguments with the highest scores. You will have a tough time elaborating on your points if you choose five different arguments to try and support. **I recommend only picking two or three main ideas and spending an entire paragraph explaining each one.** If you have five great arguments, try to combine them or twist them slightly so you can use one to support another.

The best arguments are those that you can support with strong reasons, examples, and details. While being creative certainly helps, even the most obvious arguments will earn high scores if you support them well. Each argument should have roughly two to four verifying reasons or examples, although this is not an exact science. Here is an example of the prewriting for a supporting argument and the paragraph that results:

(Prewriting) Reason for no school in the summer: Many students hold summer jobs

- *Students can save money to pay for college*
- *You begin to learn about the working world*
- *My job at the grocery store taught me responsibility*

The summer break gives students the opportunity to take on jobs which are more beneficial to them than an extra three months of school. With the rising costs of college and our country's economic state, many students rely on summer occupations to save money for their upcoming college years. In addition, summer jobs teach students valuable lessons in responsibility they will use as they move on to the "real world". Showing up late to school means a tardy slip or possibly an hour of detention; showing up late to your job could result in getting fired. Personally, my job at the local grocery store has helped greatly in my transition from a dependent adolescent to a self-sufficient man. The financial and personal gains I have made in my summer work are far more valuable than an extra three months of classes.

Notice how I stick to one main point the entire paragraph and stay on track with the supporting details. I transition between reasons and examples and do not get stuck repeating myself. Furthermore, I hint at some defense against counterarguments by comparing the consequences of being late to school and being late to work (the counterargument being that school teaches responsibility just as well as a job). This paragraph, along with an introduction, conclusion, and one or two other supporting paragraphs, would make for a very strong essay.

Here's another quick tip that I mentioned briefly earlier:

Not everything you say needs to be 100% true: OK, I confess, I never worked at a grocery store. The ACT grader will not do a background check though! In addition, I just assumed that college costs are rising; I really don't know the exact trends of the last couple years. This is not to say you should lie just for the sake of lying. Nor should you make up far-fetched facts or stories that are unnecessary, distracting, and/or suspicious. But the occasional presumed fact or borrowed story will not get you into trouble if appropriately placed.

5. *Smashing Counterarguments*

Graders like to see that you acknowledge the views of others by responding to counterarguments. At the same time, you do not want to make this a central part of your essay. Most of your essay should be dedicated to reinforcing your own points. Treat responses to counterarguments as another method to support your main points. Be careful though, you want to make sure everything still transitions smoothly. If you cannot logically fit a response to a counterargument into your introductory or body paragraphs, make it a theme of your conclusion; basically, just don't force it. Go back a page and check out the sample paragraph under Tip 4. Notice how the response to the counterargument is mixed in with other details.

Note: Your response to a counterargument does not necessarily have to be as subtle as the example in the sample paragraph. See my example under "Squash a significant counterargument" on page 78 for a more direct response to a counterargument.

6. *Ending Strongly: The Conclusion*

The conclusion is your last chance to impress the reader. A good one can make up for an otherwise average essay. There are several aspects common to good conclusions, and a few things that should be avoided. Also, there are a few standard methods to constructing conclusions. They are all listed on the next two pages.

Good Conclusions Contain:

a. A rephrasing of your thesis statement. This will reinforce your views and show the true purpose of your essay. Just do not give a word-for-word reproduction of the thesis used in your introduction. The rephrased thesis sentence can be placed anywhere in the conclusion.

b. At least three sentences. Short conclusions make it look like you ran out of thoughtful things to say. Graders will be left with a bad final impression.

c. A sense of completeness. Don't leave questions unanswered.

Avoid These in Your Conclusion:

a. Using the phrases "In conclusion..." or "To summarize..."

b. Introducing new topics. This is why you have body paragraphs. If you just came up with a great idea, sorry, it's probably too late.

c. Making your point for the first time. Sometimes students like to leave an air of mystery around their main point throughout the essay, and then drill it in during the final paragraph. While that can work in certain papers, the ACT essay is analytical and this approach will not work here.

Conclusion Strategies – Use one or a couple of these together to end strongly:

a. Summarize and synthesize. Summarizing your main arguments is a classic way to end a paper. However, simply repeating your earlier arguments will make for a boring conclusion. Try to bring your main points together ("synthesize") to make some general statements on the issue. Also, try to use new language and sentence structure when summarizing past points.

b. Make a recommendation for further action. Recommendations are a great way to end a paper, although sometimes they are not practical given the topic. Use wisely. Here is an example of a good use of recommendations, and then one that is a bit over the top:

> Good use: As we approach another school year, we should ask our educators, why are our country's young minds falling behind the rest of the world during a lazy summer break?
>
> Bad use: We should march to our state senators and tell them to mandate the summer break for the sake of our young students.

c. Give a tangible solution. Make a plea for a certain course of action. Just make sure it fits with the rest of your essay and is not coming out of nowhere. In fact, you probably want to hint at this solution during the introduction and body paragraphs. Your conclusion should never surprise the reader. Here is an example of a creative, tangible solution:

> While a summer break is best for our young students, mandatory usage of summer reading programs would force students to keep their minds active during this time off.

d. Reference your anecdote from the introduction. You are certain to wow readers if you can start a story in the introduction, go on to make your points, and then finish the story or provide commentary on it in your conclusion. This is not easy to pull off, but it is doable if you plan it out during your prewriting time.

e. Suggest the importance of your view. By taking your recommendation, what is going to happen? How is this going to change things? Why is this important? Answering any of these questions will add a lot of meaning to your essay. You can also take a passive approach to using this strategy. Sometimes you can suggest the importance of your view just by "synthesizing" your main arguments (instead of directly answering the above questions). Either way can be effective.

Note: Some of these conclusion strategies are meant for stronger writers looking for a top score. If you do not see writing as a strength for you, keep things simple and don't try to do too much. A simple summary of your main points can still earn a good score.

7. *The Final Edit*

Once your introduction, body, and conclusion are complete, read your essay over if you have extra time. Correct errors, throw in better vocabulary words, and make sure your message is clear during this review time. You probably will not have time to make any significant changes to your essay, so be confident and just "tidy up" your work.

Notes - Writing

Notes - Writing

A Last Word to Students

Congratulations on making it through The ACT Black Book. I hope you learned some valuable information for your upcoming ACT Test. Keep working hard and do your best on test day. You should have no problem conquering the ACT.

Please send any suggestions or comments you have for this book to Comments@SuperiorTestPrep.com. Your feedback helps us improve the book each year. Thank you!